10665470

The Essence of
RUMI

The Essence of
RUMI

JOHN BALDOCK

EAGLE EDITIONS

This edition printed in 2006

Published by Eagle Editions Limited
11 Heathfield
Royston
Hertfordshire SG8 5BW

Copyright © 2005 Arcturus Publishing Limited
26/27 Bickels Yard, 151–153 Bermondsey Street, London SE1 3HA

ISBN 1-84193-384-8

Printed and bound in Great Britain by William Clowes Ltd, Beccles, Suffolk

Cover image: Court of Safavid prince, from 1650 Persian manuscript
[The Art Archive/Museum of Islamic Art Cairo/Dagli Orti]

Contents

Introduction

Jalaluddin Rumi, the thirteenth-century Sufi saint and poet, was a master storyteller. One of the most frequently retold of his stories is the tale about the elephant in the dark.

Some Hindus put an elephant on show in an unlit room. Many people came to see it, but because it was impossible to see the elephant in the dark they felt it with the palms of their hands. One put his hand on the elephant's trunk, and exclaimed, 'This creature is like a drainpipe.'

Another put her hand on its ear, saying, 'It's shaped like a fan.'

A third, who felt its leg, commented, 'It's like a pillar.'

A fourth placed his hand on its back, and said, 'Really, this elephant is shaped like a throne.'

In like manner, everyone described the elephant from the part he had touched, and their descriptions differed depending on their particular standpoint, with one describing it as being crooked like an 's', another straight like an 'l'. If they had each held a candle, their descriptions would not have differed. Knowledge gained through our senses is comparable to knowledge obtained with the palm of a hand: a palm cannot extend over the whole elephant.

The eye of the Ocean is one thing, the eye of the foam another. Ignore the foam and look with the eye of

> the Ocean. All day long, flecks of foam spray up from the Ocean. You see the spray, but not the Ocean. How extraordinary!
>
> (*Mathnawi* III: 1259–71)

Originally told to illustrate the limitations of our human view of the Ocean of Reality, this story can also be applied to our personal view of Rumi. As with those who felt the elephant in the dark with the palm of their hands, our view of Rumi will be governed by whichever aspect of him we have touched, or whichever aspect has touched upon us. Yet, as Rumi himself points out in the conclusion to his story, we tend to focus our attention on the most obvious aspects of things, on the parts with which we can identify due to our own experience of life. So, for some of us Rumi is essentially a poet, for others a storyteller, a mystic or a saint, while for yet others he is their spiritual guide and teacher, known respectfully and lovingly as *Mevlana*, 'our Master'. Whatever our personal view of Rumi might be, the chances are that we see him through 'the eye of the foam' rather than 'the eye of the Ocean'. Yet the essence of Rumi's teaching is that our sensory eye can be transformed into the all-seeing eye of the Ocean.

In his writings, Rumi frequently returns to the theme of 'form' and 'essence' to illustrate the principle that our human perception of the world normally focuses solely on the outward appearance of things, on the outer 'form'. As a consequence, we tend to be unaware of the invisible aspect, the true nature or meaning of a thing, its inner 'essence'. Those, like Rumi, who have attained a unified vision of the outer and inner worlds perceive things differently. They see things from the inside out rather than from the outside in.

The theme of form and essence is also reflected in Rumi's writings in another way, since his inspiration progresses from the inner to the outer, from spiritual impulse to verbal expression. Thus, the more we are able to penetrate the outer form of his words, the closer we may come to catching a glimpse of the Source from which they came. This requires a considerable mental leap. Rumi is aware of this, for in the collection of his poetry known as the *Divan-i Shams-i Tabrizi* he advises:

> Study me as much as you like, you will not know me,
>   for I differ in a hundred ways from what you see me to be.
> Put yourself behind my eyes and see me as I see myself,
>   for I have chosen to dwell in a place you cannot see.

(*Divan-i Shams-i Tabrizi* 1372: A1:168)

The 'place we cannot see' is the Unseen, the Placeless, also known as the Non-existent. Those who dwell there have attained union with the Source of their being. They no longer exist in the normal sense of this word, having passed beyond the veil that separates us from the Divine Unity. Although they may appear to exist *in* this world, they are no longer *of* this world since their human attributes have been drowned in the Ocean of Being. For them, this world and the next have become One. In this state of being, explains Rumi, it is no longer he who is speaking to us.

> When a man becomes a vehicle for Spirit,
>   his human attributes disappear.
> Whatever he says,
>   pure Spirit is speaking,
> for the one who belongs in this world
>   speaks from one who belongs in the other.
> If Spirit can have this much effect,
>   how much greater must be the power
>   of the One whose Spirit it is!

(*Mathnawi* IV: 2112–14)

Perhaps this is the key to Rumi's enormous appeal to a twenty-first-century Western audience. Whatever we may assume his outward appeal to be, at an inner level his words resonate with the Spirit lying dormant within our soul, stirring it into life, a momentary fluttering deep within us like a foetus moving in the womb. But unless we remain alert, the ego-centred self claims this movement as its own. We find ourselves thinking, 'I had a moving experience', and with this the 'I' of the ego once more draws closed the veil of separation. Thankfully, we are able to return to Rumi's words again and again, endeavouring to approach their inner meaning through his eyes until the veil of separation becomes less opaque. When it does, we will begin to see the Path that lies ahead of us – a path which, possibly without even knowing it, we are already travelling along. Where this particular path is concerned, Rumi advises us to seek out a spiritual guide – a *shaykh* or *pir* – who has intimate knowledge of both the Path and the errings of the soul as it travels along it. If we tread the Path on our own, without a guide, it is more than likely that our ego will take control, assuring us that we are making good progress when in reality we are going nowhere.

Where does the Path lead? Of the many answers provided by the Qur'an, there are two in particular that are implicit throughout Rumi's work: *We belong to God, and unto Him we are returning* (Q 2:156), and *Wheresoever you turn, there is His Face* [or *Presence*] (Q 2:115). Moreover, as the ecstatic poetry in the *Divan-i Shams-i Tabrizi* reveals, the Path along which we travel with Rumi is none other than the Path of Love.

> We are iron filings,
> Your love is the magnet . . .

> (*Divan-i Shams-i Tabrizi* 1690: A2:211)

> Get drunk on Love, for Love is all that exists.
> Unless you make Love your business,
>   you will not be admitted to the Beloved.

> (*Divan-i Shams-i Tabrizi* 455: A1:54)

I cried out, 'Where does the drunken heart go?'
The King of Kings replied, 'Be *silent!* [7:204]
   It is going towards Us.'

(*Divan-i Shams-i Tabrizi* 898, after Schimmel,
Rumi's World, p. 44)

We shall return to the theme of Love later in this book (*see* page 180). For the moment, there is another mental leap to consider in our approach to Rumi's writings. Not only is his perception very different from our own, there are also pronounced cultural differences, for Rumi was writing in thirteenth-century Konya (now in Anatolia, Turkey). His immediate audience was steeped in the Islamic tradition and would have understood instantly Rumi's references to the Prophet Muhammad, the Qur'an, and the semi-mythical figures of Persian and Arabic culture. Moreover, Rumi was a Sufi teacher (*shaykh*), and many members of his audience were either his disciples or well acquainted with the terminology associated with the Sufi Path. However, the impact of Rumi's poetry on the Western reader is often such that these background elements are ignored, and his work is read or recited in isolation from them. The same may be said of the wider historical background of the thirteenth century. The opening chapters of *The Essence of Rumi* seek to place Rumi in this wider context.

About this book

Since this book is primarily an introduction to Rumi and the path of self-surrender, the chapters have been arranged in such a way that they progress from the outer, historical world to the inner, spiritual essence of Rumi's teaching, as follows:

- **Chapter One** offers an overview of the wider political and spiritual context of thirteenth-century Europe and the Islamic world.
- **Chapter Two** provides a brief account of Rumi's life and an introduction to his writings.
- **Chapter Three** explores Rumi's Islamic background: the life of the

Prophet Muhammad, the Qur'an and the principle tenets – the Five Pillars – of the Islamic religion. It is important to note that the Arabic word *islam* means to surrender the whole of one's being to the Divine Will, so the Islamic religion, as originally formulated by the Prophet Muhammad, can rightly be said to be the religion of surrender (or submission) to God.

- **Chapter Four** traces the historical development of Sufism, setting it at the spiritual heart of Islam. Because Rumi's audience would already have been familiar with certain aspects of the Sufi Path, his writings do not provide a systematic explanation of Sufism. This chapter therefore includes a brief explanation of the Sufi Path as well as a number of passages from Rumi's works to illustrate some of the principal aspects of Sufi thought. In his writings, Rumi makes frequent mention of some of his eminent Sufi predecessors – notably, Ibrahim ibn Adham, Bayazid Bistami and Mansur al-Hallaj – and so the chapter concludes with extracts from Rumi relating to these three.

- **Chapter Five** explores a few of the many characters who appear frequently in Rumi's writings, some of whom may already be familiar to a Western audience via the Judaeo-Christian tradition: Abraham, Joseph (son of Jacob), Moses, Mary and Jesus. For Rumi, these figures frequently take on a kind of shorthand status. For example, in his willingness to obey God's command and sacrifice his son, Abraham demonstrated his total surrender to the Divine Will (i.e., his *islam*), and so the mere mention of the name 'Abraham' carries this meaning with it. Alongside figures from the Islamic and Judaeo-Christian traditions, we find semi-mythical figures from Persian and Arab folklore such as the legendary lovers Layla and Majnun.

- **Chapter Six** explores some of the underlying meanings Rumi conveys through these and other symbols. As well as employing a large cast of characters to represent spiritual or human states of being, Rumi uses an extensive vocabulary of symbols from the natural world in his writings. As we have already seen, the 'Ocean' is shorthand for the Divine Unity, while the foam on its surface is the 'froth' of the transient, everyday world. If we wish to obtain the pearl of Divine Wisdom, we need to dive into the Ocean within us, retrieve the oyster, and open the shell. Birds, too, feature prominently in Rumi's vocabulary, for the bird symbolizes the human soul, which can fly freely or remain confined to the cage of our physical body.

- **Chapter Seven** brings us to the essence of Rumi's writings: his teachings on the nature of human being, our innate potential for spiritual enlightenment and our relationship with the Divine Unity. Furthermore, Rumi's profound understanding of both human and spiritual psychology gave him penetrating insights into the reasons why we do the things we do and think the things we think. Although they were written down over 700 years ago, the timeless wisdom offered by these insights is just as relevant today, providing the modern seeker with valuable guidance in the unfolding of his or her own spiritual evolution as they travel the Path.

- **Chapter Eight** presents a number of extracts from Rumi's prose work, a collection of seventy discourses known as *Fihi mafihi* (literally, 'In it is what is in it'). As well as teaching stories and commentaries on passages from the Qur'an, the extracts include examples of Rumi's insights into human behaviour.

- **Chapter Nine** is devoted to the second of Rumi's major works, the *Mathnawi*, a continuous poem in six volumes, written in rhyming couplets (*mathnawi* means 'couplets'), which was described by Jami, the fifteenth-century Persian Sufi, as 'the Qur'an in Persian'. The extent of the *Mathnawi*'s subject matter is vast, ranging from commentaries on verses from the Qur'an and the Traditions of the Prophet, to bawdy stories told to illustrate aspects of Rumi's teaching.

- **Chapter Ten** brings the book to a close with a selection of odes from the collection of Rumi's poems known as the *Divan-i Shams-i Tabrizi* (the Persian word *divan* means 'collection of poetry'). Rumi's encounter with Shams of Tabriz, a wandering dervish, resulted in an intense spiritual relationship that lasted until Shams mysteriously disappeared from Rumi's life as suddenly as he had erupted into it. His sudden departure and the breaking off of their spiritual communion inspired in Rumi an outpouring of ecstatic poetry in which his relationship with Shams became a tangible vehicle for the expression of the relationship between the lover (the individual human being) and the Beloved (God).

A note on the extracts from Rumi's writings

A point of debate among students of Rumi is the difference between a 'translation' and a 'version'. Strictly speaking, 'translations of Rumi' are the rendering into English from an original text by linguists, scholars or followers of Rumi with a knowledge of Persian and/or Arabic. 'Versions of Rumi' are the work of those who, in the absence of sufficient knowledge of Persian or Arabic to translate from the original, produce an interpretation based on one or more of the available translations. 'Versions of Rumi' should therefore not be considered as accurate word-for-word renderings of the original. This is particularly so with versions of Rumi's poetry. As Kabir Helminski, a shaykh of the Mevlevi order in America, points out, 'versions, whatever their value, grant more licence to the personal voice and imagination of the writer creating the versions' (Helminski, *Love is a Stranger*, p. 11).

Unless indicated otherwise, the passages from Rumi contained in the present book are 'versions of Rumi'. Because Rumi frequently developed a theme at great length, interposing verses from the Qur'an, sayings (*ahadith*; singular *hadith*) of the Prophet Muhammad, stories and anecdotes to illustrate further the point he is making, extracts from the *Mathnawi* and *Fihi mafihi* have sometimes been paraphrased or abridged. In some cases, passages from the *Mathnawi* have been rendered into continuous prose. The extracts from Rumi's three principal works included in this book also vary in style. This is intentional. Readers wishing to consult unabridged translations of Rumi's writings are directed to those referred to below and listed in the bibliography.

Following a common practice in books on Rumi, cross-references for passages from the *Mathnawi* are to the translation by Professor R.A. Nicholson, and are indicated thus: (M IV: 2062), with 'M' being the abbreviation for *Mathnawi*, 'IV' being Book IV, and '2062' the verse in

Nicholson's translation. Cross-references to passages from Rumi's
discourses in *Fihi mafihi* are accompanied by page references to the
English translations by A.J. Arberry and W.M. Thackston Jr, and are
indicated thus: (F 11: A57/T47–8), with 'F 11' being the number of the
discourse, 'A57' the page in Arberry, and 'T47–8' the pages in
Thackston. Odes from the *Divan-i Shams-i Tabrizi* are identified by
the number allocated them in Professor Foruzânfar's 10-volume
edition, *Kulliyyāt-i Shams yī Dīvān-i kabīr* (published by the
University of Teheran, 1957–67), followed by, where applicable, the
number designated in A.J. Arberry's two-volume translation of selected
poems from the *Divan* (D 2039: A2:253, where 'A2' refers to Volume 2
of Arberry). Where a version of a verse or verses from the *Divan* is
derived from a source other than Arberry, the source is given with the
relevant page number. Verses from the Qur'an are printed in italics,
followed by the number of the Surah (chapter) and the verse (for
instance, Q 8:70).

A note on the transliteration of names
Rumi wrote mainly in Persian and Arabic, both of which are
consonantal languages. That is, only the consonants (cnsnnts), the
root of the word, are written down. The same consonants may form
the root of several words, sometimes with seemingly unrelated
meanings, yet the correct sense of the word is evident to native
speakers from the context and their knowledge of the language.
Written English is very different in that the vowels are an integral part
of the written language. When Persian or Arabic words are rendered
into the Latin (or Roman) alphabet, which is the alphabet used for
English, vowels are inserted. It is at this point that variations in the
spelling of proper names and other words arise – as yet there is no
standardized system of transliteration.

Chapter One

Rumi and History

Every horse has its stable, every beast its stall, every bird
its nest. And God knows best.

(F 70: A242/T246)

The milestones that mark the course of human history can be defined
in any one of a number of ways depending on the particular aspect of
history that interests us, whether this be the wars that have been
fought, the dynastic lineage of rulers, the development of a given
religion, the social history of a people, or the sequencing of political
events. In this respect, history is like the story of the elephant in the
dark: no one can see the whole picture. And yet, to borrow Rumi's
analogy, if we look beneath the foam of history we will perceive the
swell of the Ocean; in the same way, Rumi's rare references to historical
events place them firmly within the greater context of the Divine Unity.

From a historical viewpoint, the thirteenth century in Europe and
Asia was a period of unprecedented militancy during which the Islamic
world was subjected to dramatic change. To the east, the hordes of
Genghis Khan emerged from Mongolia, conquered northern China,
and swept westwards, sacking everything in their path, including
Baghdad (1258), the seat of the Caliphate. To the west, the defeat of
the Moorish forces at Los Navos de Tolosa (1212) heralded the demise
of Muslim power in Spain. The century also witnessed numerous
bloody Crusades to the Holy Land and Egypt. Yet, at the same time,
there was a strong spiritual impulse at work in the world. The evidence
for this is to be found in the life and work of Rumi and the other saints
and mystics who lived at this turbulent time. As Rumi is often seen in
isolation from this broader background, the following condensed

overview of the European and Islamic worlds is intended to place him in a wider political and spiritual environment. I am indebted to Colin McEvedy's *Penguin Atlas of Medieval History* for much of the information in this section. However, such a brief overview will inevitably suffer from a number of omissions.

EUROPE FROM THE DEMISE OF THE ROMAN EMPIRE TO THE THIRTEENTH CENTURY

The Byzantine and Holy Roman Empires

In the fourth century CE, the Roman Empire still retained a hold over much of modern Europe and the Mediterranean, where its south-eastern borders abutted the Arabian Peninsula and the Persian Empire. In 330 CE, the Roman Emperor Constantine rebuilt the ancient Greek city of Byzantion, renamed it Constantinople, and established it as his capital. It remained the capital of the Eastern Empire when the Roman Empire was split into the Western and Eastern Empires in 395. In the fifth century, the forces of Attila the Hun emerged from Central Europe and extended their territory at the expense of the two weakened empires. The following decades witnessed the collapse of the Western Empire, whereas the Eastern Empire became a dominant force in the eastern Mediterranean. A series of conquests during the sixth century saw the Eastern Empire extend its territory westwards as far as the Iberian Peninsula. In the seventh century, the Emperor Heraclius reorganized the Eastern Empire, which had become increasingly Greek in character, and it is from this point onwards that Western historians generally refer to it as the Byzantine Empire after the ancient Greek name for Constantinople. The Empire's territory was reduced by the expansion of Islam in the eighth century, and further reduced by the Seljuk Turks' conquest of Anatolia in the eleventh century. The demise of the Byzantine Empire was completed in 1212 when the Crusaders sacked its capital, deposed the Emperor, and established the Latin Kingdom of Constantinople. Of the remnants that remained under Greek rule, the one of the most immediate significance to us was the Empire of Nicaea, which lay between the Bosporus and the Seljuk

Sultanate of Iconium. A vestige of the old Roman Empire lingered on in Anatolia, which was known as the 'Roman land' or 'Rum', from which comes the name Rumi, meaning 'from Rum'.

Meanwhile, in what had been the Western Empire, the eighth century had witnessed the conquest of most of Western Christendom by Charlemagne (c.742–814), King of the Franks, who was crowned Holy Roman Emperor in 800. On his death, the Holy Roman Empire was divided up between his three sons. By the late ninth century, the three kingdoms of France, Italy and Germany had become the dominant powers. Under Otto I (912–73), the German kingdom extended its borders to include much of modern Italy, and Otto was crowned Holy Roman Emperor in 962. The dominant position of the new Empire gave rise to open conflict between successive popes and emperors from the eleventh century onwards. In 1273, the Empire passed to Rudolf I (1218–91), a member of the Habsburg family.

Western Europe

Following the demise of the Western Empire, the frequent invasions of the Italian peninsula led to the emergence of a number of powerful self-governing city-states, the first of which were Venice, Pisa and Amalfi. Others followed. Trading links with far distant countries were not uncommon, and the Venetian Marco Polo (c.1254–1324) achieved fame through his account of his travels to China, where he is said to have served under the Mongol emperor, Kublai Khan.

By the thirteenth century, the English kingdom extended into Ireland, Wales, and much of modern France, but the English lost Normandy to the French in 1204. The defeat of the English at the battle of Bouvines in 1214 saw them lose much of the remainder of their French lands. The following year the English barons forced King John to sign the Magna Carta at Runnymede. In France, the century was dominated by the reign of Louis IX (b.1214, reigned 1226–70), who led the Sixth Crusade (1248) and died while on a later Crusade in Tunisia. Regarded as the model medieval Christian king, Louis was made a saint in 1297. The Iberian Peninsula had been conquered by the armies of Islam in the eighth century, but by the beginning of the thirteenth

century the Moors had been driven back into southern Spain. By the
end of the century, Moorish territory in the peninsula was confined to
the Emirate of Granada, home of the Alhambra (begun 1238).

Central and Northern Europe

The early history of central Europe is dominated by the great tribes of
people who were to give their names to many of the countries of
present-day Europe: including the Slavs, Huns, Magyars and Bulgars.
As the centuries passed, a number of more clearly defined realms
emerged. By the thirteenth century, the map of central Europe was
dominated to the north by the Polish principalities, at its centre by the
kingdom of Hungary, and to the south by the Bulgarian empire and
the kingdom of Serbia. In the 1240s, these lands were invaded by the
Mongol armies, but there was no lasting occupation since they
withdrew eastwards after the death of the Khan.

The marauding raids of the Norsemen and Danes in the medieval
period led to the conquest of considerable lands in western Europe –
especially in the British Isles and northern France – but by the
thirteenth century these raids had more or less come to an end
following the Christianization of the Scandinavian kingdoms.
Meanwhile, the Swedes had spread eastwards, colonising the Russian
shores of the Baltic Sea, and early in the ninth century made lengthy
incursions into Russia itself (then Slav territory), where they
established the principalities of Kiev and Novgorod. In the later ninth
century, the Russian principalities were united and the new state
expanded its lands both to the north and to the south, where they
reached the Black Sea. By the thirteenth century, the principality had
disintegrated into several smaller realms, which succumbed to the
invading Mongols (also known as the Tartars) in the 1230s.

The Crusades

Whereas the first Crusades undertaken in the eleventh century had
been conducted largely for religious motives, those of the thirteenth
century degenerated into little more than a pretext for territorial
expansion in which Christian sometimes fought against Christian. One

such was the Fourth Crusade (1202–4), which set out for the Holy Land but changed course, sacked Constantinople (1204), deposed the Byzantine Emperor, Alexius III, and established the Latin Kingdom of Constantinople. The Albigensian Crusade (1209–28), named after the town of Albi in southern France, sought to wipe out the heretical Cathars. Some 50,000 children from France and Germany set out to capture Jerusalem on the ill-fated Children's Crusade (1212). They failed to reach their destination and only a few returned home, most of those who survived being sold into slavery. The Sixth Crusade (1228–9) retook Jerusalem, which had been captured by Saladin in 1187, but lost it again to a Muslim army in 1244. The failure to regain the Holy Land led to later Crusades being directed mainly at Egypt, which, after the fall of Baghdad to the Mongols in 1258, had become the seat of the Caliphate.

Although the territorial gains of the Crusades were short-lived, the contact they provided with Islamic civilization was to have a profound influence on European culture (*see* Idries Shah, *The Way of the Sufi*, pp. 18–21, and *The Sufis*, pp. xiii–xx).

Rumi makes a rare reference to the Crusades in an ode from the *Divan-i Shams-i Tabrizi*, in which he delivers a withering response to a critic.

> O sour-faced one, you spoke evil of me in my presence, but then a vulture's beak always stinks of putrefied flesh.
> Your face bore witness to your foul words, for baseness always shows on the face of a nobody.
> I have a Friend and Beloved, so churn out your hate and venom; but be warned, the ocean was never fouled by the mouth of a dog.
> The Holy City has become inundated with Frankish pigs, yet has that brought the Holy Temple into disrepute?

> (D 1211: A1:154)

Rumi's reference to the Crusaders' occupation of Jerusalem, although little more than a passing comment, provides us with an insight into his view of historical events. He places them on a par with the abusive comments of one of his critics. This is not arrogance on Rumi's part. As we saw in the Introduction, Rumi is both aware and respectful of his spiritual station (*see* page 9). His critic clearly was not. In his response, Rumi once more draws attention to the distinction between form and essence, between the foam and the Ocean. As he says, 'the ocean was never fouled by the mouth of a dog.' Nor is it fouled by historical events.

While the rulers of Europe fought to defend or expand their domains, another, more subtle, tussle was taking place; one that concerned itself with the spiritual edification of the people. For want of a better description, I have called it a 'spiritual impulse'. It could also be described as the call of the Ocean.

The thirteenth-century spiritual impulse

At the turn of the century, the rebuilding of the cathedral of Chartres after the fire of 1194 heralded the full flowering of Gothic architecture in France, and the ensuing decades witnessed the building or rebuilding of cathedrals in the Gothic style throughout Europe: Bourges, Paris, Reims, Amiens, Beauvais, Wells, Salisbury, Canterbury, Old St Paul's, Westminster Abbey, Marburg, Cologne, Strasbourg, Siena, Burgos and many others. The thirteenth century also witnessed the flourishing of the schools of learning attached to the cathedrals, in which the teaching of theology and philosophy were influenced greatly by the works of Plato and Aristotle (the latter of which had only recently been translated from Arab sources).

A number of philosophers, mystics and saints emerged at this time in Europe, and were thus Rumi's contemporaries. In Britain, we find Roger Bacon (*c*.1214–92), the Franciscan monk, philosopher, and alchemist, known as Doctor Mirabilis for his wide-ranging skills and learning; William of Ockham (1285–1349), the philosopher and theologian, famous for the introduction of the principle of 'Ockham's razor'(the principle of the fewest possible assumptions); and the

Scottish-born philosopher and theologian, John Duns Scotus (*c.*1265–1308). In Spain, there was Maimonides (1135–1204), the Jewish philosopher; Moses de Leon (d.1305), to whom is attributed authorship of the *Zohar* (The Book of Splendour), the classic text of Jewish Kabbala; and Ibn 'Arabi (*see* 'The Islamic World' below), the great Sufi teacher and metaphysician, who was born in Murcia, southeast Spain in 1165. In Italy, Francis of Assissi (1182–1226), founder of the Franciscan Order; Thomas Aquinas (1225–74), Dominican theologian, author of the *Summa Theologica*; and Dante Alighieri (1265–1321), whose *Vita Nuova* was published around 1290. In Germany, the mystic, Mechthilde of Magdeburg (1217–82); and Meister Eckhart (*c.* 1260–1328), the influential Dominican mystic, posthumously condemned as a heretic.

The thirteenth-century spiritual impulse was not confined to Europe. It also manifested in the Islamic world. Further afield, in Japan, the Kamakura period (1185–1333) has been described as the 'golden age of Japanese Buddhism'. It was during this period that two Japanese schools of Pure Land Buddhism were founded: the Jodo-shu (Pure Land School) by Honen Shonin (1133–1212), and the Jodo Shin-shu (True Pure Land) by his disciple Shinran Shonin (1173–1263). Zen Buddhism also made its appearance in Japan at this time: the Rinzai school was introduced by Eisai (1141–1215), who built the first Zen temple in Japan in 1184, and the Soto school was founded by the great Zen Master Dogen (1200–53).

THE ISLAMIC WORLD

From the Prophet Muhammad to the thirteenth century
By the end of his life, the Prophet Muhammad had united the previously pagan tribes of the Arabian Peninsula under the banner of Islam. In the thirty years following the Prophet's death (632), his immediate successors – known as the Four Rightly-Guided Caliphs – succeeded in making considerable territorial gains with the rapid conquest of Syria, Palestine, Egypt, Cyprus, Sicily, Rhodes, parts of North Africa and many Mediterranean ports. In the process, the

Byzantine Empire was seriously weakened and the Sassanian Persian Empire was all but destroyed.

The title 'Caliph' is the Anglicized form of *khalifah* ('vicegerent' or 'representative'), and is taken from a verse in the Qur'an in which God tells the angels about His creation of Adam, saying, *I am placing a vicegerent on the earth* (Q 2:30). The Caliph was therefore the successor to the Prophet in both the temporal and spiritual sense. Dissent over the rightful succession to the Caliphate led to the murder of Imam 'Ali, the last of the Four Rightly-Guided Caliphs, who had all been close companions of the Prophet during his lifetime. The dissent was led by Mu'awiyah, head of the Ummayad clan, who was declared Caliph in 661. Mu'awiyah immediately moved the seat of the Caliphate to Damascus. The overthrow of the Ummayads in 750 saw the establishment of the 'Abbasid dynasty and the removal of the Caliphate to the new city of Baghdad, which was founded that same year.

Expansion of the Islamic Empire continued into the next century, penetrating northwards into the Volga region, eastwards into Central Asia, where the Turkish tribes were converted to Islam, and westwards into the Iberian Peninsula. At the same time, a number of Emirates and smaller Caliphates became independent, thus undermining the political unity that had been part of the legacy of the Prophet. In the tenth century, the Fatimid dynasty strengthened its position in North Africa with the capture of Egypt (969), where the Fatimids built a new capital at Cairo. Towards the end of the century, the Turkish Sultan Mahmud of Ghazna (a kingdom comprising present-day Afghanistan and north-eastern Iran) began the conquest of north-western India, and established the Ghazvanid dynasty (*see* 'Mahmud and Ayaz', page 135).

The eleventh century witnessed the rise of a new force, the Seljuk Turks, who overthrew their Ghaznavid overlords and rapidly conquered the lands to the west, up to and including Syria. Towards the end of the century, the Seljuks conquered Anatolia, destroyed the Byzantine army and pushed the borders of the Byzantine Empire back to the Bosporus. As the eleventh century ended, the armies of the First Crusade set out from Constantinople and recaptured Jerusalem

(1099), on the way creating a number of crusading states along the shores of the Mediterranean. Following in their wake, the Byzantines reoccupied some of the land they had lost earlier to the Seljuks, including Nicaea. The twelfth-century Crusades met with some initial success, but were eventually checked by Saladin, who recaptured Jerusalem in 1187, abolished the Fatimid dynasty in Egypt (1171) and founded the Ayyubid dynasty. As the century unfolded, Seljuk power declined. To the east, it lost Transoxiana (between the Oxus river and China) to the Buddhist Mongolians, while the land it had gained from the former kingdom of Ghazna was seized following a revolt by the Seljuks' Ghuzz mercenaries. In the west, the Seljuk Sultanate disintegrated into several small states. The most significant of these where we are concerned was a sultanate in Anatolia. The last vestige of Seljuk power, the sultanate took its name from its capital city, Iconium, which is better known to us as Konya.

The thirteenth century

In 1200, 'Ala'uddin Takesh, ruler of Khwarizmshah (the realm in north-eastern Persia, where Rumi was born), was succeeded by his son, 'Ala'uddin Muhammad, who set about extending his domain. By 1210, he had driven the Karikhitai out of Transoxiana and extended his borders westwards as far as the Euphrates to embrace most of Persia and much of the territory that had once been ruled by the Seljuks. 'Ala'uddin's ambition of further expansion was, however, cut short by Genghis Khan, whose forces swept westwards from Mongolia, crushing everything in their path.

In one of his rare references to contemporary history, Rumi describes the sequence of events that led up to the Mongol invasion of Persia. In a discourse in *Fihi mafihi*, Rumi recounts that some of the Mongols entered Khwarizmshah trading as cloth merchants. However, the ruler of Khwarizmshah had some of them killed, imposed taxes on others and prohibited them from entering his realm. They returned to their own king, who, on being told of their plight, withdrew to a cave and fasted for ten days, 'humbling and abasing himself'. At the end of this time, God proclaimed, 'I have heard your plea. Come forth, and wherever you go victory will be yours.' And, Rumi adds, that is what happened. When the Mongols went forth 'at God's command, victory was theirs, and they conquered the world' (F 15: A76/T67–8).

On their way westwards, the Mongols sacked Bukhara, a renowned centre of learning, and slaughtered most of its 200,000 inhabitants. Samarkand suffered a similar fate; likewise Balkh, Nishapur and other great Persian cities. The death of Genghis Khan in 1227 did not slow the chain of conquests, the climax of which came in 1258 with the destruction of Baghdad and the annihilation of the Caliphate. It is said that one million of the city's inhabitants were massacred. The effect on Islamic culture was similarly devastating. 'The Caliphate which had existed for more than six centuries became extinct at one blow. Muslim civilisation has never recovered from the devastation wrought by the Mongols . . . The awful nature of the cataclysm . . . is difficult to realise and certainly impossible to exaggerate' (Iqbal, *The Life and Work of Rumi*, p. 29). The advance of the Mongols was eventually checked by the Mamluk Turks, successors to the Ayyubid dynasty in Egypt. As a direct consequence, the centre of Muslim life moved from Baghdad to Cairo, the former capital of the Fatimid dynasty. Further west, the thirteenth century saw the reduction of Muslim power in the Iberian Peninsula.

The spiritual impulse

Where the Islamic world is concerned, the spiritual impulse could be said to have begun with the Prophet Muhammad in the seventh century, and to have been maintained thereafter by the Sufis, with each generation reaffirming the original impulse (*see* page 82). The thirteenth century was no exception and its first decades were dominated by the famed Sufi metaphysician Ibn 'Arabi (1165–1240), known as Shaykh al-Akbar (the 'greatest shaykh'). The beginning of this century also saw the introduction into India of the Chishti *tariqah* (plural *turuq*; usually translated as 'Sufi order') by Shaykh Muinuddin Chishti (*c*.1142–1236), as well as the foundation of two new *turuq*: the Shadhili *tariqah* in North Africa, founded by Shaykh Abu'l-Hasan ash-Shadhili (1196–1258), and the Suhrawardi *tariqah*, founded by Shaykh al-Suhrawardi (1144–1234) of Baghdad. The thirteenth century was also the age of the great Persian Sufi poets: Fariduddin Attar (d. 1229), Fakhruddin Iraqi (1213–89), Sa'di of Shiraz (c.1215–92), Shabistari (1250–1320) and, of course, Jalaluddin Rumi.

Chapter Two

The Life of
Jalaluddin Rumi

I have relinquished duality and seen the two worlds as
   one;
One I seek, One I know, One I see, One I call.

(after Nicholson, *Selected Poems from the Divani
Shamsi Tabrizi*, p. 127)

What is known of Rumi's life comes from three principal sources: his
own writings and those of his immediate contemporaries, such as his
son, Sultan Walad; the hagiographies written by those who came after
him; and the work of modern scholars.

The most reliable of these are the first and last of the three, for
hagiographers – those who write the lives of saints – have a tendency
to embellish or gloss the facts in order to emphasize the saintly nature
of their subject. Rumi's best-known hagiographer – Shams al-Din
Ahmad Aflaki (d.1360) – was no exception. Nonetheless, his *Manaqib
al-'arifin* (Legends of the Saints), which recounts the lives of Rumi and
his circle, is the source of some of the anecdotal stories in the
following pages. In his Preface to James Redhouse's 1881 translation of
Aflaki's *Legends*, Idries Shah explains that to get the best from these
stories 'one has to bear in mind the premises which underlie the
operation of a Sufi school. Not the least of these is the well-established
technique of proffering stories, legends and so on not necessarily for
teaching purposes, but also often to test the mentality and reactions of
the hearer.' The same principle can be applied to the events and
stories recounted by Rumi.

THE FORMATIVE YEARS

Khorasan

Jalaluddin Rumi was born on 30 September 1207 in Balkh, in the province of Khorasan in northern Persia (now Afghanistan), where his father Baha'uddin Walad was a respected scholar and mystic. At least, that is how most accounts of Rumi's life begin. Recent scholarship suggests otherwise: at the time of Rumi's birth, his father is now said to have been living some 250 km north-east of Balkh, in the small town of Wakhsh, situated in modern Tajikistan. Moreover, Baha'uddin Walad was a minor preacher and jurist with mystical leanings, rather than the prestigious figure portrayed by Aflaki and others (Lewis, *Rumi*, pp. 47, 92; Schimmel, *Rumi's World*, p. 11).

How did the confusion over Rumi's birthplace arise? Franklin D. Lewis suggests that after the Walad family had emigrated to Anatolia, Baha'uddin and Jalaluddin perhaps specified Wakhsh as their place of origin when talking with fellow émigrés from Khorasan. (Rumi makes a brief reference to Wakhsh in M IV: 3319.) But, since it was unlikely that Anatolians would have heard of this small town, they 'apparently allowed the people of Anatolia to believe that they came from Balkh, one of the major cultural centres of the day'. The reputation of Balkh would thus have provided the local Turks with a point of reference. It would also have enhanced the Walads' prestige (Lewis, *Rumi*, p. 48).

Various explanations are given for the Walad family's departure from Khorasan. Some say Baha'uddin left because of a premonition about the impending Mongol invasion. Others say his departure was due to the hostility of Fakhruddin Razi, the philosopher and influential courtier of the Khwarizmshah – a hostility whose roots lay in the persistent and widespread dissension between philosophers and Sufis (*see* page 173). The story goes that the relationship between the philosopher and the mystic became so strained that Baha'uddin decided to go into exile. These explanations are all combined in Aflaki's account of events, according to which Baha'uddin began to preach against the Khwarizmshah and some of his courtiers, urging them to practise the principles of Islam. In return, the courtiers

intrigued against him, accusing him in front of the shah of having
designs on the throne. The shah offered him the throne, but
Baha'uddin refused, saying that he was a poor recluse, unconcerned
with worldly honours. Moreover, he would be willing to leave the
country to put the shah's mind at rest. Before leaving, Baha'uddin gave
a public address at the great mosque in the presence of the shah,
during which he predicted the coming of the Mongols, their invasion
of the country, and the destruction of Balkh. He also foretold that the
Mongols would drive out the Khwarizmshah, who would then seek
refuge in the Roman land (the lands of the old Roman Empire, referred
to as 'Rum' by Arab and Persian writers), and there he would be killed
(Aflaki, *Legends of the Sufis*, p. 2).

According to Aflaki, at the time that Baha'uddin emigrated
westwards his family comprised a daughter (Fatima Khatun), an eldest
son (Husayn), both of whom probably stayed behind in Khorasan,
along with Baha'uddin's elderly mother. The family members he took
with him included his wife (Mu'mine Khatun), and two sons,
Jalaluddin and 'Ala'uddin (Lewis, *Rumi*, p. 46). The latter was the elder
of the brothers by two years, having been born in 1205.

The actual reason for Baha'uddin's departure from Wakhsh –
which Aflaki likens to the Prophet Muhammad's emigration from
Mecca to Medina (*see* page 65) – remains uncertain. So does the date.
Lewis suggests that the Walad family was still in Wakhsh in September
of 1210, but had moved to Samarkand by 1212, the year the city was
taken by the Khwarizmshah (Lewis, *Rumi*, p. 55). Rumi would have
been about five years old at the time. Much later in life, he recalled the
siege of Samarkand in *Fihi mafihi*, where he recounts how a beautiful
woman who lived in his neighbourhood had been saved from harm by
placing her trust in God.

> In the part of the city we were in there was an extremely
> beautiful woman whose beauty was without equal in the
> entire city. I heard her say, 'O God, how could You let me
> fall into the hands of these wicked men? I know You would
> never allow such a thing, and so I put my trust in You.'

> When the city was sacked and its inhabitants were taken
> prisoner, that woman's maids were also taken into captivity,
> but she remained unharmed. In spite of her great beauty,
> no one so much as laid a finger on her. The moral of this is
> that whoever entrusts himself to God will be free from
> harm, and that no one petitions God in vain.

(F 45: A181/T180–1)

Tradition relates that when the family left Samarkand they passed
through Nishapur, where they visited the famous Sufi poet Fariduddin
Attar. Attar, who appeared to have been deeply impressed by the
young Jalaluddin, presented him with a copy of his *Asrar-nama* (Book
of Secrets). As Baha'uddin set off again with Jalaluddin following
behind, Attar is said to have remarked: 'There goes a river dragging a
mighty ocean behind it.' But, according to Lewis, the story of this
meeting 'must be dismissed as a legend', since its first appearance
dates from the fifteenth century. Although Rumi had an intimate
knowledge of Attar's writings, making frequent reference or allusion to
them in his own works, he makes no mention of such a meeting having
taken place. Instead, Lewis suggests that the meeting was 'imagined by
later readers' to show how 'the mystical torch is passed on from
generation to generation' (Lewis, *Rumi*, pp. 64–5).

From Khorasan to Anatolia

From Khorasan, the travellers journeyed on to Baghdad, where it is
suggested they arrived in 1217 and stayed for about one month (Lewis,
Rumi, p. 66). Aflaki relates that as Baha'uddin approached the city the
Caliph sent out a deputation to greet him, headed by Shahabuddin al-
Suhrawardi, the great Sufi shaykh and founder of the Suhrawardi
tariqah. Baha'uddin turned down the Caliph's gift of money, and
refused to visit him, but accepted an invitation to preach in his
presence in the congregational mosque. In his sermon, Baha'uddin
admonished the Caliph for his corrupt way of life, warning him that he
would meet an ignominious end in the forthcoming Mongol invasion.
Aflaki adds that it was while the family was in Baghdad that news

reached the city of the siege and sack of Balkh. The Mongols had reduced this ancient centre of learning to little more than a pile of rubble. In doing so, they had destroyed 12,000 mosques and 14,000 copies of the Qur'an, killed 15,000 students and professors of jurisprudence, and slaughtered 200,000 adult male inhabitants (Aflaki, *Legends of the Sufis*, p. 3).

Aflaki's inference that the destruction of Balkh occurred around the time of the Walads' visit to Baghdad serves to illustrate the difficulties encountered by scholars when trying to compile an accurate account of the family's movements from the hagiographies, for the sack of Balkh took place in 1220, by which time the Walads were already far away in eastern Anatolia. Prior to reaching Anatolia, however, they had undertaken the pilgrimage to Mecca and also visited Damascus and Aleppo. It has been suggested that the Walads arrived at Aqshahr, near Erzincan (on the upper reaches of the Euphrates) in eastern Anatolia, between late 1217 and early 1218 (Lewis, *Rumi*, p. 70). There Baha'uddin is said to have taught for four years in a college (*madrasah*) built for him by the wife of Fakhruddin Bahramshah, the local ruler. After the death of his patrons, Baha'uddin and his family moved on to Laranda (Karaman in present-day Turkey) (Aflaki, *Legends of the Sufis*, pp. 3–4).

Laranda and Konya

The town of Laranda was situated in the central Anatolian province of Rum (the 'Roman land' from which the name 'Rumi' derives), which was ruled by Seljuk sultans from their capital in Konya (ancient Iconium). According to Aflaki, the Walads remained there for about seven years, during which time Baha'uddin taught in the *madrasah* founded by the local governor. The period in Laranda was also marked by two deaths, a marriage, and two births in the Walad family: 'Ala'uddin (the elder of the two sons travelling with Baha'uddin) and Mu'mine Khatun (Baha'uddin's wife and mother of Rumi) both died; Rumi came of age, and married Gevher Khatun, the daughter of Sherefuddin of Samarkand – a marriage that may have been prearranged, since Gevher's mother had been a prominent female disciple of Baha'uddin (Lewis, *Rumi*, p. 71); and, in due course, Rumi's young wife gave birth to two sons – 'Ala'uddin, named after Rumi's recently deceased older brother, and Sultan Walad, who was named in honour of his grandfather. While sources seem to disagree over which of the two was born first, they generally concur that the boys were born about a year apart.

While in Laranda, Baha'uddin received an invitation from the Seljuk ruler, 'Ala'uddin Kay-Qubad, to teach in Konya, where the family settled in 1229 when Rumi was twenty-two. Baha'uddin taught in the *madrasah* in Konya until his death, two years later, in February of 1231, when he was some eighty years old.

Baha'uddin Walad

The verbal portraits painted of Baha'uddin by hagiographers and modern scholars present two strongly contrasting images. Aflaki and others portray him as an important, highly respected spiritual teacher and mystic, whose genealogy befitted his spiritual station. According to Aflaki, Baha'uddin's mother was a princess – the daughter of 'Ala'uddin, the Sultan of Khwarizmshah – while his father was a descendant of Abu Bakr, the First Caliph and close companion of the Prophet. The marriage of Baha'uddin's father (Jalaluddin al-Khatibi) to the princess had been foretold in the dreams of four people – Baha'uddin's father, the Sultan of Khwarizmshah, the Sultan's daughter, and his vizier – in which each was told by the Prophet that Jalaluddin should marry the princess. Nine months after their marriage, they had a son whom they named Baha'uddin. Aflaki continues:

> When adolescent, this latter was so extremely learned that the family of his mother wished to raise him to the throne as king; but this he utterly rejected.
>
> By the divine command, as conveyed on the selfsame night, and in an identical dream, to three hundred of the most learned men of the city of Balkh, the capital of the kingdom where he dwelt, those sage doctors unanimously

conferred upon him the honorific title of *Sultan al-'ulama'* (King of Clerics), and they all became his disciples.

(Aflaki, *Legends of the Sufis*, pp. 1–2)

Again according to Aflaki, Baha'uddin's migration from Khorasan to Konya resembled a triumphal progress, for whenever he passed through a town or city along the route deputations of nobles and spiritual leaders were sent out to greet and honour him. Baha'uddin is also said to have preached in the great mosques to large congregations, and to have berated local rulers face-to-face over their corrupt ways. Yet, the image of Baha'uddin presented by modern scholars is that of a minor preacher and jurist with mystical leanings.

Whichever of the two images is closest to the reality, Baha'uddin's mystical tendencies are evident from the *Ma'arif*, a collection of his writings and teachings, in which he described his spiritual experiences and visions. It is also clear that Rumi became imbued with his father's mysticism, for in his own writings also he touches on many of the subjects dealt with in the *Ma'arif* (Lewis, *Rumi*, pp. 85–6). (For a summary of the views expressed by Baha'uddin in the *Ma'arif*, *see* Lewis, *Rumi*, pp. 86–90.)

The last word on Baha'uddin is best left to Rumi himself, for the high regard in which he held his father is illustrated by the story he tells about him in *Fihi mafihi*. (In the story, the Arabic word *qiblah* refers to the 'direction of prayer' – the direction of the Kaaba in Mecca, towards which Muslims face when praying; the word *hadith* denotes a saying attributed to the Prophet Muhammad.)

> One day his [Baha'uddin's] companions found him totally absorbed in contemplation. When the time for prayer arrived, some of his disciples called out to the Master that it was the hour of prayer. The Master took no notice, so they stood up and started to pray. However, two disciples remained with their master and did not stand for the prayers. Now, one of the disciples praying – a man named Khwajagi – saw with the eye of the heart that all those who

were standing behind the one leading the prayers had
turned their backs to the *qiblah*, whereas the two disciples
who had remained with the Master had turned towards it.
Since the Master's sense of self had been annihilated,
consumed in the Light of God – the meaning of the *hadith*,
'Die before you die' – he had become the Light of God.

(F 3: A24/T13–14)

Burhanuddin Muhaqqiq al-Tirmidhi

Two significant events occurred in Rumi's life during the period
immediately following the death of Baha'uddin. First, he succeeded his
father as teacher in the *madrasah* in Konya. This was either in
accordance with his father's will, or at the request of Sultan 'Ala'uddin,
or out of respect for the wishes of Baha'uddin's followers (Iqbal, *The
Life and Work of Jalaluddin Rumi*, p. 61). The second event was the
arrival in Konya, a year after Baha'uddin's death, of one of his former
pupils from Khorasan, Burhanuddin Muhaqqiq, who took charge of
Rumi's spiritual development – a task that may have been assigned to
him by Baha'uddin before the latter left Khorasan (Iqbal, *The Life and
Work of Jalaluddin Rumi*, p. 64).

The arrival of Burhanuddin was more in the manner of a reunion,
for he and Rumi had known each other in Khorasan. Moreover, in
taking charge of Rumi's spiritual education, Burhanuddin assumed a
role that he had had some nineteen or so years previously when he had
been tutor to the infant Rumi. Aflaki relates that Burhanuddin often
told how he would frequently lift up the young Jalaluddin and carry him
on his shoulders. 'But now,' he would add, 'Jalal has attained such a
high spiritual station that he carries me up' (Aflaki, *Legends of the Sufis*,
p. 19).

Burhanuddin sent his pupil to Aleppo to further his studies. He
also sent him to Damascus, where Rumi is said to have spent either
four or seven years, although he may have returned to Konya from
time to time during this period. He also instructed him in the spiritual
practices of the Sufis, such as fasting, and it was after a particularly
rigorous fast in Kayseri (ancient Caesarea), during which Rumi is said

to have performed three forty-day fasts in succession, that Burhanuddin pronounced him 'perfect in all the sciences, outer and inner, human and spiritual' (Aflaki, *Legends of the Sufis*, p. 20). Burhanuddin developed Rumi's education in other areas, too. Through Baha'uddin Walad, Rumi had become acquainted with the work and teachings of the great Ghazali (d. 1111; *see* pages 84–5). Now, through Burhanuddin, he was introduced to the work of the Sufi poet Sana'i of Ghazna (d. 1131) who had been the first to use the *mathnawi* (rhyming couplet) form as a vehicle for spiritual expression and instruction.

Baha'uddin Walad's patron in Konya, 'Ala'uddin Kay-Qubad, the Seljuk Sultan of Rum, died in 1237, and was succeeded by Ghayathuddin Kay-Khusru II. If Rumi was still in Damascus when the sultan died, he would have felt the need to return to Konya, both to pay his respects to the new ruler and to secure his tenancy of his father's old position of teacher at the *madrasah* (Lewis, *Rumi*, p. 114). It was around this time that Burhanuddin left Konya for Kayseri, where he was to spend the remainder of his life. A possible explanation for his departure is that Rumi, out of respect for his teacher, would have felt it inappropriate to accept the role of teacher or shaykh while Burhanuddin was still present in Konya. Burhanuddin's withdrawal to Kayseri would have enabled the 30-year-old Rumi to assume his new role (Lewis, *Rumi*, pp. 116–17).

Shams-i Tabrizi

When Rumi took over his father's old post as teacher in the *madrasah* in Konya, he seemed 'destined for a career of modest distinction as an expositor of the faith and the sacred law' (Arberry, *Discourses of Rumi*, p. 5). But, on a November's day in 1244, the 37-year-old Rumi was on his way home from the *madrasah* when he was accosted by an itinerant dervish, Shams of Tabriz. Accounts differ as to exactly what happened at this first meeting between the two men, but it was a life-changing experience for Jalaluddin. The most frequently repeated account of what happened is that told by Aflaki.

> One day, as he [Shams] was seated at the gate of an inn,
> Rumi came by, riding on a mule, in the midst of a crowd
> of students and disciples on foot. Shams arose, advanced
> and took hold of the mule's bridle, addressing Rumi in
> these words, 'Exchanger of the current coins of deep
> meaning, who knows the Names of God! Tell me, was
> Muhammad the greater servant of God, or Bayazid
> Bistami?'
>
> Rumi answered him, 'Muhammad was incomparably
> the greater – the greatest of all prophets and saints.'
>
> 'Then,' rejoined Shams, 'how is it that Muhammad
> said, "We have not known Thee, O God, as Thou ought to
> be known," whereas Bayazid said, "Glory unto me! How
> great is my glory."?'
>
> On hearing this question, Rumi fainted. On regaining
> his senses, he took the questioner to his home.
>
> (Aflaki, *Legends of the Sufis*, p. 21)

Aflaki recounts two versions of the meeting, of which the above is the
shorter. In the longer version, Rumi answers differently, saying that
Bayazid's spiritual thirst was quenched after one drink, and so he
stopped seeking. But Muhammad's thirst was never quenched. He
went on seeking, seeing more and more of the Divine. It was for this
reason that he said, 'We have not known Thee as Thou ought to be
known.' At these words, it was Shams who fainted, not Rumi.
(Helminski, *The Rumi Collection*, p. xx. A similar account by Jami, the
fifteenth-century Persian Sufi and poet, is given in Thackston, *Signs of
the Unseen*, pp. ix–x.)

The name 'Shams' means 'Sun', and this is what Shams became
for Jalaluddin: the dawn rising of a spiritual sun that precipitated an
ascent into the higher realms of consciousness. Rumi said of their
meeting, 'What I thought of before as God, I met today in a person.' It
is said that the two men spent days, even months, together in a state
of mystical communion, dead to the outer world. But the sudden and
total disappearance of Rumi, their spiritual master, from the life of

Konya, its mosque and *madrasah*, aroused resentment among his followers, some of whom threatened Shams.

In February of 1246, Shams disappeared just as suddenly as he had appeared fifteen months earlier. Perhaps sensing imminent danger, he had fled to Damascus. In the spiritual vacuum left by Shams' disappearance, Rumi the scholar became Rumi the poet, and his heightened state of consciousness poured itself forth in ecstatic verse expressing the mystical love of Lover and Beloved. Some months later, news arrived that Shams had been seen in Damascus. A letter was sent asking him to return to Konya. Shams refused. More letters followed and were met with the same reply. Eventually, Sultan Walad, Rumi's son, was sent to bring the errant dervish back.

Shams returned to Konya in May 1247, but it was not long before old resentments resurfaced, culminating in the 'dolorous event . . . that terminated the life of Shams' (Aflaki, *Legends of the Sufis*, p. 98). One evening in December of 1247, so the story goes, Rumi and Shams were together when there was a knock at the door, and it was announced that a dervish who had travelled a long distance was asking to see Shams. Shams left the room and was never seen again. It is said that he was attacked and stabbed to death by a gang of assailants led by Rumi's son, 'Ala'uddin. Rumi heard Shams cry out, but by the time he arrived on the scene Sham's body had already been carried away into the night. Some bloodstains on the cobbles in the courtyard were the only clue as to what might have happened to the Sun of Tabriz.

This account of the 'dolorous event' was first related by Aflaki, and has been repeated in slightly differing forms ever since. Yet it was first written down more than seventy years after Shams had disappeared (Lewis, *Rumi*, p. 189). Its reliability is therefore questionable, and the real explanation for Shams' second disappearance may be altogether more prosaic.

For many years, Shams had travelled widely, seeking out the most spiritually evolved men of his time. Having visited many such men, he asked God to guide him into the presence of a living saint. He was told in a dream that the saint he was seeking was in Anatolia. When the time was right, he set off for his encounter with Rumi (Lewis, *Rumi*, p. 153). A possible explanation for both of Shams' disappearances is provided in the collection of his writings known as the *Maqalat*, which Franklin Lewis describes as 'the single most important primary source (aside from Rumi's own writings . . .) for understanding Rumi's spiritual transformation and his teachings' (Lewis, *Rumi*, p. 137). When Shams had returned to Konya after his first period of absence, he wrote in the *Maqalat* that he had gone away for the sake of Rumi's spiritual development. To this end, he would 'go away fifty times', since separation 'matures and refines' (Lewis, *Rumi*, p. 182). Ample evidence for the transformation brought about by Rumi's separation from Shams is provided by the outpouring of poetry in the *Divan-i Shams-i Tabrizi*, for the sober religious teacher and spiritual guide became Love's ecstatic poet.

I was dead, and came back to life. I wept, and became laughter. Love overpowered me, and I became the power of Love.

My eye has seen its fill, and my soul feels no fear. I'm lion-hearted, I shine like Venus.

He said, 'You're not mad, you're not fit for this house.' I became a madman, and was bound in chains.

He said, 'You're not drunk. Go, you don't belong here.' I went and got drunk, inebriated with joy.

He said, 'You're not slain, you're not drowned in joy.' Before his life-giving face I lay down, dead.

He said, 'You're a clever so-and-so, drunk on doubts and fantasies.' I became everybody's fool, and gave my self away.

He said, 'You've become a candle, the focal point of the community.' I am neither a candle, nor part of a community, I've become smoke wafting in the air.

He said, 'You're a shaykh and leader, a guide along the way.' I am neither shaykh nor leader, I am a slave to your command.

He said, 'You've wings and feathers, I need not

give you wings to fly with.' Out of yearning for his wings
and feathers, my wings were clipped and plucked.

   Future prosperity said to me, 'Don't go, don't get
anxious; out of grace and generosity I am coming to you.'

   Old love said to me, 'Don't leave my bosom.'
I said, 'I won't. I am at peace, and here I will remain.'

                                          (D 1393: A1:170)

THE MATURE YEARS

Rumi's spiritual relationship with Shams can be likened to the
workings of a blacksmith's forge, for it is as though he were a piece
of iron heated to white heat in a fire and then hammered into the
required shape. What followed next was a period of refinement,
during which Rumi's powers as poet and teacher soared to new
heights.

Salahuddin Zarkub

Following the disappearance of Shams, the close spiritual relationship
that Rumi had formerly enjoyed with the Sun of Tabriz now manifested
itself in his relationship with Salahuddin Zarkub, the goldbeater. Like
Rumi, Salahuddin had been a pupil of Burhanuddin Muhaqqiq.
Tradition relates that they met again some years later, when Salahuddin
was working in the goldsmiths' market in Konya. Rumi passed by and
began to dance in a turning, whirling movement to the sound of the
goldsmiths' hammers coming from Salahuddin's workshop. From that
moment, Salahuddin became his close companion, although Rumi's
relationship with him was less intense than with Shams. The marriage
of Rumi's son, Sultan Walad (by then a widower), to Salahuddin's
daughter further strengthened the bond between the two men, and
they remained close companions until Salahuddin's death in 1258.

   Salahuddin took over the position previously held by Shams in
another way, too. For the resentment that Rumi's followers had shown
towards Shams now turned itself against Salahuddin. From all

accounts, Salahuddin served as Rumi's deputy, overseeing the organization and discipline of the Master's close followers. It seems, however, that many objected to this because Salahuddin had no formal training in the religious sciences. Yet Rumi clearly held him in very high regard, as evidenced by a discourse in *Fihi mafihi* in which he springs to the defence of Salahuddin and reprimands a certain Ibn Chavish for backbiting. The discourse also offers us an insight into the position held by Salahuddin within the community of followers.

> Ibn Chavish used to say to me, 'The Shaykh of Shaykhs, Salahuddin, is a great man. From the day I entered your service, I never heard him refer to you except as "Our Master", and I never heard him once change this mode of address.' Have Ibn Chavish's own selfish ambitions rendered him blind? Now he says that Shaykh Salahuddin is nothing. What wrong has Shaykh Salahuddin ever done him, apart from seeing him falling into a pit and saying, 'Don't fall into the pit'? He said this out of the compassion he feels for him above all others, yet Ibn Chavish detests this compassion . . .
>
> Shaykh Salahuddin counsels you for your own good, but you attribute ulterior motives to his compassion and advice. Why should a man like him have other motives or harbour enmity where you are concerned? . . . Shaykh Salahuddin is the root of spiritual joy. Since the ocean of joy is within him, how could he hate anyone or wish them harm? He speaks out of compassion for all God's servants. What other motive would he have for dealing with the likes of these 'locusts' and 'frogs'. How can a man of such stature be compared with the likes of these miserable wretches?

> (F 22: A106–7/T99–100)

Husamuddin Chelebi (Çelebi)

While Salahuddin was still alive, another close disciple of Rumi's rose to a position of prominence within the Sufi community – known as the

Mevlevi, a term derived from Rumi's honorific title of *Mevlana* (our Master) – that had established itself around Rumi. This was Husamuddin Chelebi, who had first met Rumi while a young boy and was still in his teens when he became one of his disciples. At the time of their first meeting, Husamuddin appears to have been a member of one of Konya's urban youth guilds. With their 'code of civic virtue and mercantile morality', these organizations provided an alternative to the more spiritually-oriented Sufi orders, but they also displayed some of the characteristics of a 'militia or mafia-like gang'. The shaykhs of these confraternities were addressed as 'my brother' (Arabic *akhi*) by the members, but the term 'Akhi' used to describe these orders in Anatolia derives from a Turkish word for 'generosity'. Husamuddin's father, the head of a branch of one of the Akhi orders, was known as Akhi Tork. Husamuddin was still in his teens when his father died; on his appointment as his father's successor, he took his branch of the brotherhood to join Rumi. However, one particular Akhi order – the Akhi Evren – was noted for its rivalry with Rumi and the Mevlevi (Lewis, *Rumi*, p. 216).

Aflaki describes one particular confrontation between Rumi and a group of Akhi brethren that occurred following the death of a certain shaykh in Konya. The Sultan appointed Husamuddin as the shaykh's successor, and arranged a lavish entertainment to mark the occasion of Husamuddin's installation at the deceased shaykh's school. Rumi himself carried his young friend's carpet to the school, and spread it out on Husamuddin's new seat. However, a certain Akhi Ahmed, who was annoyed by Husamuddin's appointment and had a reputation as a troublemaker, grabbed the carpet and gave it to one of his companions to throw out of the building, saying: 'We will not have this man installed here as shaykh.' In the ensuing uproar, several leaders of the Akhi order who were present drew their swords. Bloodshed seemed imminent, but Rumi intervened. He addressed the crowd, reproached them for their inappropriate behaviour, and then told them the following anecdote:

A certain shaykh from Samarkand, whose name was Abu-
'l-Lays, travelled for some twenty years with the purpose of
furthering his studies, some of which time he spent in
Mecca. Eventually he set out on the journey home,
preceded by his reputation and a number of disciples.

When he arrived at the outskirts of his home town,
he went down to the river to perform his ablutions. There
he encountered a group of women washing clothes. One
of them, an old woman, came over to him, studied his face
at close quarters, and then called out: 'Why, if it isn't little
Abu-'l-Lays come home again! Quickly, girls, go and tell the
family.'

The shaykh rejoined the group travelling with him,
gave the order for the animals to be loaded up at once as
they were to depart immediately for Damascus. When he
was asked the reason for this sudden change of mind, he
answered: 'My people still think of me as "little Abu-'l-
Lays", and so they will treat me with familiarity, and
consider me of little account. They will thus commit a
serious error, for it is a duty incumbent on everyone to
honour the learned and the wise. To respect them is to
show reverence to the apostle of God, and to revere him
is to serve the Creator.'

Now, if the truth be known, his father had always
called him 'little Abu-'l-Lays' when he was a child. But
strangers would not understand this term of endearment in
that way; they would think of it as being too familiar, and
thus likely to bring the divine displeasure down on the city
and its inhabitants. It would not have been consistent with
true compassion to allow such an eventuality to occur.

(Aflaki, *Legends of the Sufis*, pp. 105–7)

By way of conclusion, Aflaki says that when Rumi had delivered this
constructive reprimand he 'left the college barefoot, and in high
dudgeon', pursued by various dignitaries who sought to intercede. But
Rumi refused to be pacified, and he refused to be reconciled with Akhi

Ahmed, who had sparked off the fracas. He adds, however, that Akhi 'Ali, the son of Akhi Ahmed, later became a follower of Sultan Walad.

After the death of Salahuddin Zarkub, Husamuddin rose to the position of *khalifah* (assistant, or deputy) and became Rumi's constant companion. It was at his request that Rumi composed a short 'teaching' poem for the benefit of his close followers. Eighteen verses long, this poem – now known as the *Song of the Reed* (*see* page 181) – was destined to become the opening of the *Mathnawi*, for when Rumi presented it to Husamuddin he said, 'From now on I will recite, and you will write the rest'. The dictation of 'the rest', which extends to six books, probably began in 1260 or 1261 and, apart from one or two interruptions, continued until 1273.

Rumi's 'Wedding Night'

In the autumn of 1273, Rumi fell ill. The Seljuk Sultan, his vizier and other officials came to visit him on his sickbed, and two imperial physicians were in constant attendance. On 17 December, at the age of 66, Rumi left this world and was reunited with his Lord, an occasion which is referred to by his followers as his 'wedding night', or 'night of union'. His passing shook Konya, a spiritual equivalent of the earthquakes that had shaken the town earlier that winter. Aflaki relates that during the earthquakes Rumi had commented that the earth was hungry for 'a fat morsel', and that she would soon receive one (Aflaki, *Legends of the Sufis*, p. 84).

Rumi was mourned by the entire city of Konya, and his funeral was attended by people of all ages, races and religions: Turks, Greeks, and Arabs; Muslims, Jews and Christians. When non-Muslims were asked why they were attending the funeral of a Muslim sage and saint, they replied that 'they had learnt from him more of the mysteries shrouded in their scriptures, than they had ever known before, and they declared, "If you Muslims hold him to have been the Muhammad of his age, for us he was the Moses, the David, and the Jesus of our time."' (Aflaki, *Legends of the Sufis*, p. 87.)

It was Rumi's wish that Husamuddin be his spiritual successor, and in the years immediately following Rumi's death he continued to guide the Mevlevi community according to the ideas and principles of its late master. When Husamuddin died in 1284, he was succeeded by Rumi's son, Sultan Walad, who was instrumental in founding the *Mevleviyya*, the Mevlevi Order of Sufis.

In the centuries since, Rumi's tomb has been visited by people from all walks of life, from humble pilgrims to heads of state, and the adjoining *dergah* (convent) of the Mevlevi Order received numerous endowments. During the reign of Suleyman the Magnificent (1520–66), the *semahane* (a ceremonial hall where the *sema* or 'whirling' was done) was built adjoining Rumi's mausoleum, which was also the burial place of his father and of his immediate successors. Cells for the dervishes were added under later rulers, and fresh endowments led to the founding of new *dergahs* throughout Anatolia and further afield. In 1925, following Ataturk's ban on Sufi Orders in Turkey, the mausoleum and its surrounding complex of buildings were turned into a museum. With its dervish cells, large kitchen, and its adjoining *semahane*, the museum gives an idea of the training undertaken by those who wished to be initiated into a Sufi Order.

RUMI'S WRITINGS

Rumi's mother tongue was Persian, but like most Muslims he acquired a knowledge of Arabic as a child while learning to recite the Qur'an. Following his family's migration to Anatolia, he also learnt Turkish. His intimate knowledge of these languages is reflected in his writings, which although written mainly in Persian contain passages in Arabic and Turkish. Although his three major works have been translated into many languages, they are generally referred to by name as *Fihi mafihi*, the *Mathnawi* and the *Divan-i Shams-i Tabrizi*.

Fihi mafihi
Written during the last years of Rumi's life, *Fihi mafihi* is in prose and contains the transcripts of discourses given by Rumi to his close followers. Translated literally, the title means 'In it what is in it', which can be further rendered as 'You get out of it what is in it for you'. It is

generally accepted that the transcripts were taken down by a scribe while the discourse or conversation was taking place, and may have been corrected later by Rumi himself. Among the subjects he discourses on are the outer and inner worlds, duality and nonduality, the Sufi path to enlightenment, and the relationship between the pupil and his/her spiritual mentor. The discourses themselves are enlivened with anecdotes and stories, and in many instances they also incorporate rudimentary lessons in human and spiritual psychology.

The Mathnawi

The *Mathnawi* grew out of Husamuddin's request for Rumi to write a short 'teaching' poem. The work, which owes its title to the Persian for 'couplet' or 'distich', takes the form of an extended poem, over 25,000 verses long, and comprises six books, each with a prose introduction. It is an exceptional work, not only in length but also in style and content, for it blends traditional tales, parables, anecdotes and legends about the Sufi saints with stories about the prophets, and commentaries on the Prophetic Traditions and passages from the Qur'an. Sometimes the stories and commentary flow smoothly one into the other, at other times a story is interrupted by another story which is told to illustrate or underline a certain point before the narrator returns to the first story as though we had never left it. All are woven together to create a framework for Rumi's teaching. In a passage in the *Mathnawi*, he describes his book as follows:

> Every shop stocks a different kind of merchandise: the
>   *Mathnawi* is the shop for spiritual poverty.
> A shoe-shop has fine leather: if you see any wood, it is
>   the shoemaker's last on which he forms the shoe.
> A draper's shop has silk and fine cloth: if you see any
>   metal, it is the draper's measuring stick.
> Our *Mathnawi* is the shop for Unity: if you see anything
>   other than God in it, it is an idol.

(M VI: 1525–8)

The Divan-i Shams-i Tabrizi

Also known as the *Divan-i Kabir*, this collection of Rumi's lyrical poetry, much of which was written under the name of Shamsuddin of Tabriz, comprises over 3,000 *ghazals* (odes), and 2,000 *ruba'iyyat* (quatrains). The poems in the *Divan* cover a span of almost thirty years, from shortly after Sham's arrival in Konya to Rumi's death in 1273, and are an impassioned celebration of the Divine Unity; or, perhaps more specifically, of Love. Not to be confused with sentimental or emotional love (which are but pale reflections of it), the Love of which Rumi speaks is the glue that binds together the Divine Unity. In binding us to the Source of our being, Love has the power to heal our sense of separation from the Divine Unity. It is also our means of escape from the twin 'prisons' of our physical body and the material world.

Rumi's spiritual station was such that for him the material and spiritual worlds were one. His words – whether spoken or written – served as a bridge between the two:

> When a man becomes a vehicle for Spirit,
>   his human attributes disappear.
> Whatever he says,
>   pure Spirit is speaking,
> for the one who belongs in this world
>   speaks from one who belongs in the other.

(M IV: 2112–13)

Rumi is able to see the value of words from the perspective of both worlds. Aware that his audience might simply take his words at face value, he encourages us not only to listen attentively to what he says but also to digest it fully. In the following poem from the *Divan*, he likens his poetry to freshly baked bread: it needs to be eaten while still warm. Moreover, the organ we need to use for digesting his poetry is the heart, not the head. If we use our head, the poetry will be like stale bread; or worse, we will be feeding on what our minds imagine him to be saying, rather than on the meaning behind his words.

My poetry is like Egyptian bread: night passes, and you can
    no longer eat it.
Eat it while it is still fresh, before the dust settles on it.
It belongs in the heart's warm climate – in this world it
    dies of cold.
For a brief moment it wriggles like a fish out of water. A
    moment later it is lifeless.
If you eat it believing it to be fresh, your imagination will
    have to work overtime.
And what you'll be feeding on is your imagination, not
    these old words, my friend!

(D 981: A1 / 125)

Rumi expands on this theme in a discourse recorded in *Fihi mafihi*,
where he explains the relationship between words and mental images.
He also defines the uses and limitations of words.

> The world of mental images is broader than the world of
> sensibilities and concepts because all concepts are born of
> mental images. Likewise, the world of mental images is
> narrower than the world that gives birth to mental images.
> This is as far as verbal understanding can take us, but reality
> itself cannot be expressed through words.
>
>   'Then what use are words?' asked someone.
>
>   Words are useful because they stimulate you and set
> you searching, but what you are searching for cannot be
> attained through words. If it were so, there would be no
> need for striving and self-annihilation. Words are like seeing
> something moving in the distance: you run towards it to see
> what it is that is moving, not so that you can see the thing
> through its movement. Inwardly, human speech is the
> same. It stimulates you into searching for the meaning, even
> though you cannot see it in reality.

(F 52: A202/T203)

In another discourse from *Fihi mafihi*, Rumi makes a surprising admission. Employing the verbal imagery of food and cooking – a theme that appears often in his writings, as in the above reference to Egyptian bread and the often-told story of the chickpea in the cooking-pot (*see* page 93) – he likens reciting poetry to preparing a dish of tripe for his guests.

> My temperament is such that I do not wish to cause anyone distress . . . I abhor the thought that when friends come to visit me they might become bored, so I entertain them by reciting poetry. Aside from this, why would I bother with poetry? By God, I detest poetry. There is nothing worse. It is like having to thrust my hands into tripe and clean it because it is what my guests want to eat. This is why I recite poetry.
>
> (F 16: A85–6/T77)

Away from the kitchen, the word 'tripe' has become a synonym for 'rubbish', and this may colour our understanding of the point Rumi is making with his culinary analogy. Poetry may be the language of the heart or soul, but because it uses physical words it is very much of *this* world, even when it seeks to express the reality of the *other*. Yet Rumi knows that words have the power to stimulate us into searching for the elusive reality that lies beyond the confines of the world of physical form. To borrow a saying from the Zen tradition, his words are like 'fingers pointing to the moon'.

At a time when we in the Western world spend many hours in fitness clubs exercising our physical bodies, Rumi's writings provide much needed exercise for our neglected hearts and souls. With characteristic compassion for his fellow beings and a profound understanding of human nature, he encourages us to stretch ourselves, expanding our inner capacities in order to attain a higher state of being. When the occasion calls for it, however, he can be almost brutally blunt, even scathing, in his endeavour to awaken us to our potential to attain a state of consciousness other than the one in which we are governed by the whims of ego and the desires of our physical body. In one of his most telling and frequently quoted analogies, he likens our human predicament to 'an angel's wing tied onto an ass's tail' (F 25: A118/T111; *see also* page 144). This predicament will prevail until we abandon our dualistic mode of consciousness and, like Rumi, experience the two worlds as One.

While his poetry may stimulate us into seeking higher reality and higher truths, Rumi himself was acutely aware that human words are of limited value when compared with the Word of God. He expressed this nowhere more forcefully than in the opening lines of an ode from the *Divan* (*see* page 223, for the complete poem).

> If my words are not worthy of Your lips,
>   take up a rock and crush my mouth.
>
> (D 2083: A2:260)

Rumi's understanding of the inadequacy of words to express Divine Truth is paralleled by his emphasis on the value of silence, for he knows that only by curtailing our verbal outpourings – both inner and outer – will we be able to hear and respond to the Divine Will. Furthermore, as Afzal Iqbal remarks, 'a stage arrives when silence becomes the height of eloquence!' (Iqbal, *The Life and Work of Jalaluddin Rumi*, p. 198.) To both these ends, many of Rumi's poems from the *Divan* end with a call for silence that echoes the Qur'anic instruction, *listen in silence* (Q 7:204).

> Listen! Clam up your mouth and be silent like an oyster
>   shell,
> for that tongue of yours is the enemy of the soul, my
>   friend.
>
> (D 1082: A1:137)

> When the lips are silent, the heart has a hundred tongues.
> Be silent! How much longer do you want to try Him?
>
> (D873: A1:111)

Silence! To complete the poem our speaking King is
    coming.

(D 837: A1:106)

Yesterday, as day was breaking, the Beloved said to
    me . . .
'You are a drop of My Ocean. Why are you still spouting
    words?
Come, drown in the Ocean, and fill the soul's oyster shell
    with pearls.'

(D1022: A1:130)

. . . One world here, another there – I am sitting on the
    threshold.
Only those on the threshold know the eloquence of
    silence.
Enough has been said. Say no more. Hold the tongue.

(D 1789: A2:222)

Chapter Three

Rumi and Islam

A room with no windows is Hell. To open up windows
is the primary function of religion.

(M III: 2404)

As a child, Rumi would have learnt about the life of the Prophet
Muhammad, learnt the Qur'an by heart, acquired a knowledge of the
religious law (*shari'ah*), and performed the obligatory rituals
applicable to children. Even at an early age, his understanding of Islam
would have been all the greater due to the influence of his father,
Baha'uddin Walad. The years Rumi spent under the tutelage of his
father's disciple, the Sufi Burhanuddin Muhaqqiq, and the periods of
study in Damascus and Aleppo deepened his understanding of outer
(exoteric) Islam as well as its inner, mystical meaning. This
understanding deepened further during his years as a teacher in the
madrasah at Konya. The degree to which Rumi had assimilated both
the outer and inner aspects of the religious sciences by the time he
was thirty-seven is borne out in the intensity of his relationship with
Shams of Tabriz. For if Rumi's knowledge and understanding had been
any less than it was, Shams would never have travelled to Konya to be
in the presence of this 'living saint' (*see* page 37). When poetry began
to pour forth from Rumi's pen and he sought to give verbal expression
to the highest mystical states, it was only natural that he should draw
on the well of religious and spiritual knowledge he had accumulated
since childhood.

One of the first things a Muslim learns is that the Prophet
Muhammad is *the Messenger of Allah and the Seal of the Prophets* (Q
33:40), for what was revealed to the Prophet completed the cycle of

revelation that had begun with Abraham. The Qur'an also tells us that what was revealed to the Prophet Muhammad was the same as had been revealed to Abraham, Moses and Jesus: *Nothing is said unto thee [Muhammad] that was not said to the Messengers before thee* (Q 41:43). This timeless revelation is that *the only religion with Allah is submission [al-islam] (to His Will and Guidance)* (Q 3:19). This is the inner essence of all religions. Our human disagreements and differences over religion stem from religion's outer *form*, not from its *essence*. Later in the same surah, the Qur'an provides a succinct response to our tendency to argue about the outer form of religion: *Abraham was not a Jew, nor a Christian; he was an upright man who had surrendered himself to God* (Q 3:67).

For Muslims, the Prophet Muhammad is the model of spiritual perfection, and he left clear signposts for those who wish to follow him on the path of submission to the Divine Will. But, as with the teachings of all religious leaders, his teachings are open to two interpretations: the literal and the mystical; the outer form and the inner meaning. If we wish to understand the inner meaning of the life of the Prophet and the principal tenets of Islam, we could have no better teacher than Rumi. As an example of this we can take the Divine Tradition (*hadith qudsi*), 'But for thee, I would not have created the heavenly spheres.' (A similar principle is expressed in the West in variations on the sentence, 'The human being is the pinnacle of God's creation.') The Divine Tradition, which was addressed to the Prophet Muhammad, may present difficulties for those of us still entrapped in our ego-bound prison, given the high status it bestows on Muhammad and, by extension, to those human beings who attain a similar state of spiritual perfection. Rumi provides the following enlightening commentary in *Fihi mafihi*.

> God says, 'But for thee, I would not have created the heavens.' 'I am God' is the same thing, for it means 'I created the heavens for Myself.' It is saying 'I am God' in another way, with another metaphor.
>
> (F 11: A57/T47–8)

THE LIFE OF THE PROPHET

The Young Muhammad

The Prophet Muhammad was born in 570 in Mecca into the Hashim clan of the Quraysh tribe, one of the many nomadic Arabic-speaking Bedouin tribes that occupied the Arabian Peninsula. In contrast to the monotheistic religions of the neighbouring Byzantine and Persian Empires, the Arabs had a pantheon of pagan deities. Shrines to these deities were scattered throughout the peninsula, but the focal point of worship for pre-Islamic Arabia was the massive cube-shaped shrine of the Kaaba, dedicated to *Allah*, the High God of the Arab pantheon, which stood at the heart of an ancient sanctuary in Mecca. The Kaaba was also the setting for an annual pilgrimage (*hajj*) lasting several days, during which hostilities between warring tribes were suspended as Arabs from all over the peninsula made their way to Mecca to perform the traditional rites and rituals.

Before the seventh century had run its course this ancient sanctuary was to become the focal point for the emergent monotheistic religion of Islam, which, like Judaism and Christianity, traces its origins back to Abraham. The Qur'an tells how the foundations of the Kaaba were raised by Abraham and Ishmael (Q 2:125ff.), at the place where Abraham had made ready to sacrifice Ishmael, his son by Hagar, his slave. At the time of Muhammad's birth, the Quraysh were guardians of the sanctuary at Mecca, having abandoned their nomadic way of life several generations earlier. The Quraysh were also highly successful traders, and had turned Mecca into one of the most important cities in Arabia. Having been orphaned at an early age – both his parents had died before he was six – the young Muhammad was brought up by his grandfather 'Abd al-Mutallib. During the *hajj*, 'Abd al-Mutallib provided food and water for the pilgrims. He was also responsible for the upkeep of the Well of Zamzam (from which Hagar had obtained water during her desert sojourn with Ishmael), and so the young Muhammad would have acquired an intimate knowledge of the religious beliefs of the pagan Arabs. His early spiritual inclination is evidenced in the event known as the 'Splitting Open of the Breast' or the 'Breast Washing'.

THE SPLITTING OPEN OF THE BREAST (*SHAQQ AS-SADR*)

One day Muhammad was playing with some children when the Angel Gabriel appeared. Gabriel took hold of Muhammad, pushed him to the ground, split open the child's breast, took out his heart and cleansed it of a dark substance. The angel then replaced Muhammad's purified heart, healed his breast, and went on his way. This event, which occurred while his mother was still alive, emphasizes the importance of the heart as a spiritual organ. It also symbolizes the removal of the dark clouds of ignorance that veil the heart. With the veil of human ignorance removed, the purified heart becomes the 'source of impeccant [infallible] conduct thereafter' (Danner, *The Islamic Tradition*, p. 41). The ensuing perfect conduct of the Prophet has become the model for all true Muslims.

The supreme spiritual importance of the heart is expressed in a famous saying (*hadith*) of the Prophet, 'God says, "My heaven cannot contain Me, nor can My earth, but the heart of My believing servant can contain Me."' And again, in another *hadith*, 'The heart of man is the Throne of God.' Or, as Rumi explains, 'The heart is with Him – indeed, the heart is He.' (M I: 3489) For Sufis, the heart is likened to a mirror, and the purifying or polishing of the heart signifies not only the erasure of ignorance, but also the erasure of everything that veils the eye of the heart; in a polished heart we see nothing but God. (In Rumi's time, mirrors were made of metal and required polishing to remove any rust.) Rumi takes up this theme in the story of the Chinese and Greek painters (*see* page 94):

> They [the Sufis] have polished their hearts until purified of greed, desire, envy, and hatred. A pure heart is without doubt like a polished mirror, open to receive an infinite number of images . . . Such is their state of purity that they receive an infinity of images from the heavens, the stars, and the void, as though God were seeing through their eyes.'

> (M I: 3485, 3499)

When Muhammad was eight years old he went to live with his maternal uncle, Abu Talib, who, like Muhammad's grandfather, was connected with the religious rituals of the Meccan sanctuary. He was also a merchant, and when Muhammad was some twelve years old Abu Talib began to take him on trading trips, sometimes lasting for several months. As the young Muhammad gained in years his impeccable conduct in business earned him a reputation for honesty, and he became known as the Trusted One (*al-Amin*).

The Quraysh had not found the transition from nomadic poverty to sedentary affluence easy, for their new position brought with it a decadence in which traditional tribal values were replaced by an unbridled pursuit of worldly wealth. The clans and family units within the tribe fought each other for a share of the riches, which led to considerable inequalities of wealth; previously the more affluent members of the tribe had seen it as their duty to care for the poor. These changes did not go unnoticed by Muhammad, who saw that events were leading to the disintegration of both tribal and social structures.

Muhammad: Messenger and Prophet

THE QUR'AN

As the years passed, Muhammad took to meditating for long periods in a cave on Mount Hira, outside Mecca. It was there during a retreat in the month of Ramadan in 610, when he was about forty years old, that he received his first revelation in the form of a dramatic visitation from the Archangel Gabriel. It was night, and Muhammad was either asleep or in a deep meditative state when the angel came to him and commanded, 'Recite!' (*iqura!*, from which comes *Qur'an*, meaning 'recitation'). When Muhammad protested, saying, 'I am not a reciter,' the angel took him in a powerful embrace, holding him ever tighter until both his breath and his strength had been squeezed from him. Then the angel released him, and once more uttered the command, 'Recite!' Again Muhammad protested, 'I am not a reciter.' (A reciter or *kahin* was someone who claimed to utter prophetic oracles while in an ecstatic trance. Muhammad was protesting that he was *not* one of these people.) Gabriel took hold of him again and embraced him hard a second time, releasing him when he was on the point of exhaustion, and commanded, 'Recite!' Again, he protested, 'I am not a reciter.' For a third time the angel took him in an overpowering embrace, saying

> *Recite in the name of your Lord Who created –*
> *Who created humankind from a clot of blood!*
> *Recite, for your Lord is the Most Bountiful One,*
> *Who taught by the Pen,*
> *Who taught humankind what it did not know!*

(Q 96:1–5)

In that moment began the descent of the Qur'an and Muhammad's mission as Prophet and Messenger. Islamic tradition holds that on this particular night – a night known as the Night of Power (*laylat al-qadr*) – the entire Qur'an descended into the spiritual heart of the Prophet. It was to take many more revelations over the remaining twenty-three years of the Prophet's life for this 'vertical' descent to be transmitted 'horizontally' – that is, for the entire Qur'an to be expressed in physical words. As Rumi comments, the descent of the Qur'an eclipsed everything that had previously been written.

> The myriad of books of poetry that existed were put to shame at the word of the illiterate one [the Prophet Muhammad].

(M I: 529)

Rumi was not the first to describe the Prophet Muhammad as 'the illiterate one' (*ummi*, meaning 'unlettered one'). It was how the Prophet had traditionally been described, because his knowledge came from the source of all knowledge, the Universal Intellect. Rumi explains the meaning of *ummi* in a passage in *Fihi mafihi*, in which he also defines the relationship between the partial intellect and the Universal Intellect, a theme to which he frequently returns.

Muhammad was not called 'unlettered' because he was
unable to write or because he was ignorant of the sciences.
He was called 'unlettered' because for him writing and
wisdom and the sciences were innate, not acquired. Is a
person who can inscribe characters on the moon unable to
write? What was there in the world that he did not know,
since everyone learns from him? What can the partial
intellect possess that is not possessed by the Universal
Intellect? . . . The partial intellect has the capacity to learn
but it needs to be taught, and the teacher is the Universal
Intellect.

(F 38: A151/T148)

Rumi's intimate knowledge of the Qur'an manifests itself in his
writings, either in his commentaries on certain passages or in the
frequent quotation of, or allusion to, Qur'anic verses. Moreover, as
Rumi points out in the first of the two passages from *Fihi mafihi*
quoted below, we need to be aware that the Qur'an has both an outer
and an inner meaning. In the second passage, he sets out a method of
approaching the Qur'an so that its inner meaning is revealed.

Everyone has their own way of approaching things. The
Qur'an is a two-sided brocade. Some people enjoy one
side and some the other; yet they are both right because
God wishes that both groups of people derive benefit from
it. It is like a woman who has a husband and a baby: each
derives pleasure from her in a different way. The baby's
pleasure comes from her breast and her milk; the
husband's from intimacy and intercourse. Those who are
children of the Path 'drink milk' – that is, they derive
pleasure from the literal meaning of the Qur'an. But those
who are mature know of another kind of enjoyment and
have a different understanding of the inner meanings of the
Qur'an.

(F 44: A173/T172)

The Qur'an is like a modest bride: although you pull aside her veil, she does not show you her face. The reason your study of the Qur'an brings you neither joy nor mystical revelation is because it rejects your attempt to remove its veil. The Qur'an has tricked you, showing itself to be ugly. It is as though it is saying, 'I am not that beautiful bride.' For the Qur'an is able to show itself in whatever form it desires. But if instead of tugging at its veil you seek its good pleasure; if you water its field and tend it from afar; if you try to do what pleases it, then it will show you its face without any need for you to tug at its veil.

Seek the people of God! *Enter thou among My servants! Enter thou My Paradise!* [Q 89: 29–30].

God does not speak to everyone, just as the kings of this world do not speak to every weaver. They appoint ministers and officials through whom people can gain access to them. In the same way God has appointed certain servants, so that whoever seeks God is able to find Him through them. All the prophets have come for this reason alone: they are the way [to God].

(F 65: A236–7/T240)

Sometimes Rumi's advice is altogether more succinct:

The whole Qur'an is a commentary on the sins of carnal souls.
Read the Book! Open your eyes!

(M VI: 4862)

In another, potentially controversial, passage from the *Mathnawi*, Rumi warns against being led astray by the Qur'an. Yet, as he goes on to explain, it is not the Qur'an that has the potential to lead us astray, but our perverse desire to see it as an end in itself.

Many people have been led astray by the Qur'an:
by clinging to the rope it offers, they have fallen into the well.
The fault is not with the rope, you perverse person,
you didn't want to get to the top [of the well].

(M III: 4210–11)

The metaphor of the well alludes to the story of Joseph, the son of
Jacob, whose jealous brothers threw him down a well. For Rumi,
Joseph's escape from the well symbolized the soul breaking free from
the imprisoning confines of the human body. The same idea is
frequently expressed through one of Rumi's favourite metaphors, that
of a bird imprisoned in a cage. He employs it in the following passage
from the *Mathnawi*, in which he describes the Qur'an as the means by
which the soul may attain its freedom.

Flee to God's Qur'an and seek refuge in it, for there you
will meet the spirits of the prophets.
The Book describes the spiritual states of the prophets,
those fish in the Divine Ocean of Majesty.
If you read the Book and yet are not receptive to it, what
will you gain from meeting with saints and prophets?
But if you are receptive to the stories you read in it, your
soul-bird will fret within its cage.
A caged bird that seeks not to escape from its prison,
does so out of ignorance.
The only souls to have escaped from their cages are the
prophets, who are praiseworthy guides.
Their voices bring us the sound of faith from the Beyond,
saying, 'This is your path to freedom.
This is how we escaped from the confines of the cage,
there is no other way.'

(M I: 1537–44)

THE KAABA

One of the principal rites during the annual pilgrimage to Mecca in pre-Islamic times was the circumambulation of the Kaaba, the cube-shaped House of Allah that stood at the centre of the sanctuary in Mecca. This rite had both literal and symbolic significance, for it served as a reminder that Allah was at once the spiritual centre and physical circumference of life. However, in placing their own material success at the centre of their lives, Muhammad's tribe, the Quraysh, had chosen to ignore the inner significance of this ancient rite of orientation.

Knowing that his message of *islam* – the submission of one's whole being to the Divine Will – would not be well received by the proud Quraysh, Muhammad refrained from preaching publicly for three years. When his teaching first came to the attention of the Quraysh, they assumed it to be just another moneymaking cult to add to the many already exploiting the Kaaba and the sanctuary for material gain. All this changed in 613, when Muhammad began to preach publicly, calling upon the Meccans to reject their pagan religions and surrender to Allah, the One and Only God.

Muhammad also called for the purification of the Kaaba through the removal of its pagan idols, for Allah had commanded, *Purify My House* (Q 2:125). The Kaaba would thus be returned to its original purpose, which was for the worship of Allah alone. In other words, polytheism (*shirk*) would give way to monotheism (*tawhid*). However, the Western understanding of polytheism (*poly*, 'many'; *theos*, 'god') and monotheism tends to be in the narrow sense of 'many gods' and 'one God', whereas the sense inferred by the words *shirk* and *tawhid* is rather different. '*Tawhid* (Divine Unity) . . . is the recognition that the Divinity, *Allah*, is the One who has no second, no associate, no parents, no offspring, no peers.' (Danner, *The Islamic Tradition*, p. 4.) *Shirk*, the opposite of *tawhid*, means to attribute to any being or thing an existence that is either outside or independent of the Divine Unity. For example, in the Qur'an, Allah asks, *Have you seen those who made gods of their own passions?* (Q 25:43). By extension, our perceived separation from the Divine Unity is itself an act of *shirk*.

Like the Breast Washing, the purification of the Kaaba has a
similar symbolic meaning. But whereas the Breast Washing symbolizes
the purification of the heart by Divine Intervention, the purification of
the Kaaba signifies a conscious surrender to the Divine Unity.

While the response of the Quraysh to Muhammad's demand for
the Kaaba to be purified of its idols was predictably hostile, his
teaching continued to gain acceptance among the smaller clans.
Matters came to a head in 616, when Muhammad used his position as
one of the guardians of the Kaaba to deliver his message to the larger
audience of tribesmen who had come from all over Arabia to worship
in the sanctuary.

The Kaaba remains the focal point of the annual pilgrimage to
Mecca. It is also the 'direction of prayer' (*qiblah*) towards which
Muslims face when praying, for, as it says in the Qur'an, *We have seen
thee [Muhammad] turn thy face to heaven. Now We shall make thee
turn towards a* qiblah *that will please thee. Turn thy face towards the
sacred Mosque [the Kaaba]; wherever ye may be [O Muslims], turn
your faces towards it* (Q 2:144). (*See* 'Prayer', page 71.)

Rumi expresses the inner meaning of the Kaaba in succinct terms
in a discourse in *Fihi mafihi*.

> The meaning of the Kaaba is the heart of the prophets and
> the saints, the locus of God's revelation, of which the
> physical Kaaba is but a branch. If there is no heart, of what
> use is the Kaaba?
>
> (F 44: A174/T172)

THE NIGHT JOURNEY AND ASCENT

One evening Muhammad was by the Kaaba, 'in a state between
sleeping and waking', when Gabriel appeared to him and told him to
mount Buraq, a wondrous winged beast. Buraq took him to Jerusalem,
to the site of the ruined Temple of Solomon, where all the prophets
were gathered. Muhammad led them in prayer, and then Buraq carried
him up to Heaven. While in Heaven, the Voice of God informed

Muhammad about the obligatory prayers he and his followers would be required to perform.

The Night Journey from Mecca to Jerusalem (*al-isra'*) and Muhammad's Ascent to Heaven (*al-mi'raj*), which are described in the Surah 17 of the Qur'an and in many Prophetic Traditions, are commemorated in the annual festival of the Night of Ascent (*laylat al-mi'raj*).

The event also has an inner, mystical meaning, for the horizontal movement undertaken in the night journey from Mecca to Jerusalem corresponds to the 'dark night of the soul', the process of self-annihilation that is the necessary prerequisite before the vertical ascension of the spirit can take place. For Sufis, the *mi'raj* is 'the prototype of the mystic's own spiritual ascension to *Allah* via that ray of the Spirit connecting his soul to the Divinity' (Danner, *The Islamic Tradition*, p. 48).

The use of expressions associated with physical movement to describe what is essentially an inner, mystical occurrence can be confusing, however, for they imply that the dimensions of time and space are involved, or that we have to go somewhere or do something. Junayd, an eminent ninth-century Sufi, avoided the use of such terminology when he defined the spiritual ascension as 'the return of man to his origin, so that he will be as he was before he came into being.'

In this extract from the *Mathnawi*, Rumi refers to the ascended state as 'non-existence'. He also deals with the potential confusion that may arise from the use of the word 'ascension'.

> The Prophet said, 'My ascension is not to be
> declared as being superior to that of Jonah.
>   My ascension was up to heaven and his was down
> below [in the belly of a fish], because closeness to God is
> beyond reckoning.
>   Proximity to God is not to go up or down.
> Proximity to God comes when you escape from the
> prison of existence.

What place is there for "up" and "down" in non-existence? There is no "soon" or "far" or "late" in non-existence.'

(M III: 4512–14)

In another passage from the *Mathnawi*, Rumi likens the state of non-existence to Buraq, the wondrous beast on which the Prophet ascended to heaven.

If you join yourself to those who make the ascent, non-existence is the Buraq that will carry you aloft.

Not like the ascent of an earthly being to the moon, but like the ascent of sugar-cane to sugar.

Not like the ascent of vapour to the sky, but like the ascent of an embryo to intelligence.

The Buraq of non-existence is a wondrous steed! If you become non-existent, it will transport you to true existence.

(M IV: 552–5)

THE EMIGRATION (*HIJRAH*)

By around the year 620, Muhammad found himself increasingly threatened by the powerful Quraysh. In the meantime, a number of people from Yathrib – an oasis town some 400 km to the north of Mecca – had come into contact with Muhammad and heard his teachings. In 622, Muhammad and his Meccan followers were invited to migrate to Yathrib, where they would be given protection, and shortly afterwards Muhammad's followers began to slip away northwards. By the September of that year, the only Muslims remaining in Mecca were Muhammad and his closest companions. They, too, were ready to leave but the Quraysh were determined to stop them. To evade his persecutors, Muhammad left Mecca and headed south, in the opposite direction to Yathrib, accompanied by Abu Bakr, one of his oldest and closest followers. The men hid for three days in a cave on Mount Thawr, an hour's journey to the south of Mecca, until it was safe to head northwards to Yathrib. In the months following Muhammad's arrival in Yathrib the first Islamic community (*umma*) was formed, and in time the town came to be known by another name: *madinat al-nabi*, Medina, the City of the Prophet.

As we have already learned, Aflaki likened Baha'uddin Walad's emigration from Wakhsh to Konya to the Prophet's migration from Mecca to Medina (*see* page 31). As with all historical events, however, migration from one place to another has an underlying spiritual significance. As Martin Lings explains, 'That the Prophet and his closest companions should have migrated from Mecca to Medina was a cosmic necessity so that the orientation could take on . . . the added intensity of the turning of an exile towards his home.' (Lings, *What is Sufism?*, p. 36) The physical exile referred to here has its spiritual counterpart in our perceived separation from God. Similarly, the physical orientation towards the Kaaba in Mecca, the home of the Prophet, has its counterpart in a conscious inner orientation towards God, our spiritual home. The principle by which migration and exile inspire within us a longing to return to our true home is encapsulated in the *hadith*, 'Love of one's country is part of the Faith'. This *hadith* and the theme of migration both feature in Rumi's story of the three fish (*see* page 211).

THE HOLY WAR (*JIHAD*)
The year of the *Hijrah* (622) had seen the emigration of the Prophet and his followers from Mecca to Medina. It was not long before the Islamic community at Medina came under armed attack by the Quraysh, and so that same year saw the launch of *jihad*. Usually translated as 'Holy War', *jihad* is derived from a root verb meaning to 'strive', 'struggle' or 'exert'. In its outer (exoteric) sense, *jihad* refers to the defence of Islam and the Islamic community, whereas its inner (esoteric) sense refers to self-purification and the 'war' against the ego or lower self. The order of priority in these two types of *jihad* was defined by the Prophet in a remark to his companions as they returned home after a battle: 'We are returning from the lesser holy war to the

Greater Holy War.' They were returning from the conflict with their outward enemies to face the conflict within themselves.

Early skirmishes with the Quraysh soon gave way to full-scale warfare, and by the end of the decade the Prophet had succeeded in uniting the Bedouin tribes of the Arabian Peninsula. In 630, he marched on Mecca with an army of 10,000. The city capitulated, and the pagan idols in the Kaaba were destroyed.

In 632, the Prophet made what is now known as the 'Pilgrimage of Farewell', the first full Islamic pilgrimage to Mecca, during which he established the traditional rituals that have been followed by Muslims ever since. Shortly after his return to Medina he was taken ill and passed away in June of that year. (*See* 'The Islamic World', page 23, for a brief outline of the events that followed the death of the Prophet.)

By the time he passed from this world, the Prophet had ensured that his followers were provided with the weapons needed to succeed in the Greater Holy War. These were the Qur'an, the Sunnah of the Prophet, and the Five Pillars of Islam.

THE FIVE PILLARS OF ISLAM

The Prophet Muhammad not only set a practical example for what was required of Muslims in their outer and inner lives, he also left them with clear instructions. This combination of example and instruction is known as the Sunnah of the Prophet, or the Prophetic Norm. This gives the religion of Islam a unique quality: 'of all the major religions still extant, Islam is the only one that is essentially the same now as it was in the days of its founder.' (Danner, *The Islamic Tradition*, p. 50)

From its earliest days, Islam has had a strong oral tradition. The memorization and transmission of the Qur'an has been accompanied by a similar memorization and transmission of the actions and sayings of the Prophet. Known as Prophetic Traditions, these actions and sayings were collected together after his death. The recorded statements or *ahadith* (singular, *hadith*) that form the basis of the Sunnah fall into two kinds: those spoken by the Prophet on his own authority (*hadith nabawi*), and those in which the Prophet serves as the mouthpiece of Allah (*hadith qudsi*). As with the Qur'an, the *ahadith* have both an outer and inner meaning. The relationship between these two – that is, between the outer and inner worlds – is itself expressed in a *hadith* of the Prophet.

> The Law (shari'ah) is my words,
> the Path (tariqah) is my actions,
> and the Truth (haqiqah) is my inner states.

The Law (*shari'ah*) relates to the laws that govern the way we conduct ourselves in the outer world. It provides the outer framework within which both the individual and society may evolve towards inner awakening and higher consciousness. The Truth (*haqiqah*), from the same root as *al-Haqq* (one of the Names of God), refers to an immutable inner reality. These two realities – the outer and inner worlds – affect the way we both perceive and experience life. They are also related to our organs of sense perception: the outer world to the gross physical senses, the inner world to the subtle spiritual senses. If we approach the outer world from the viewpoint of the inner, its meaning and spirit are immediately evident. If we approach the outer world from its own viewpoint, we remain in ignorance of its inner meaning. What we have is simply a literal interpretation of the outer reality. Hence the need for the spiritual Path (*tariqah*), which binds together the otherwise dualistic realities of the outer and inner worlds, and leads us to the Truth.

Rumi's commentary on the *hadith* quoted above is to be found in the Prologue to Book V of the *Mathnawi*.

> The Law is like a lamp showing you the way. Without a lamp, there is no going forward. When you join the way, your progress along the way is the Path. And when you reach your journey's end, that is the Truth. Thus it is said, 'If the Truth were manifest, the Law would be nothing.' . . .
> The Law may be compared to learning the theory of medicine. The Path translates theory into practice through

regulating your diet and taking certain remedies. The Truth
is the attainment of everlasting health without recourse to
theory and practice. When a person dies to the life of the
world, the Law and the Path fall away from him, and only
the Truth remains . . .

The Law is knowledge, the Path is actions, and the
Truth is attainment to God.

(M V: Prologue)

These three – Law (*shari'ah*), Path (*tariqah*) and Truth (*haqiqah*) – can
also be applied to the intention with which believers practise the Five
Pillars of Islam, the obligatory practices that must be performed by all
Muslims: the Creed, the obligatory prayers, alms-giving, fasting and
pilgrimage. The mere performance of these practices does not of itself
mean that one is of a spiritual inclination. What counts is the inner
intention behind the practices, and the intention will differ depending
on whether they are performed according to the letter of the law, as a
way to the Truth, or by one who has attained union with God.

In the West, there is a habit of making life more complicated than
it really is by 'thinking' about the reason for doing things, rather than
just doing them with intention. In so doing we have become like the
philosophers who appear in a passage from the *Mathnawi* in which
Rumi discusses the approach to prayer. Commenting on this passage,
Afzal Iqbal says:

Most of those destined for Paradise are simple God-fearing
men. The clever ones are caught in the mischief of
philosophy, the simple ones perform their duties and save
themselves and the society from discord. They do not
know the philosophy of the poor-tax but they pay it; they
do not split hairs about the motives and meanings of
prayers, they simply say their ritual prayer. The philosopher
kills himself thinking; the more he thinks, the less he finds.

[M VI: 2356–7] (Iqbal, *The Life and Work of
Jalaluddin Rumi*, pp. 223–4)

Rumi refers to the intention behind the practice of the Five Pillars in a passage from the *Mathnawi*, in which his comments are characteristically blunt: one is either a hypocrite or a true believer.

> Whatever human beings may do, they are constantly
>   mimicked by the ape who studies their behaviour.
> The ape thinks it's doing the same thing, but how would
>   that perverse creature know the difference?
> Some people are moved to act on God's command, and
>   some out of perversity (may their heads be covered
>   with ashes!).
> Hypocrites pray alongside sincere believers out of
>   perversity, not humble supplication.
> In prayer, fasting, pilgrimage and alms-giving, faithful and
>   hypocrites alike enjoy victory and defeat.
> To the faithful in the end goes victory; to the hypocrite
>   goes defeat in the next world.
> While both appear to be playing the same game, in reality
>   they are leagues apart.
> Each proceeds to his appropriate dwelling place; each
>   lives up to his name.
> Call him a true believer, his soul rejoices. Call him a
>   hypocrite, he bursts into flames.

> (M I: 282–90)

The Creed (Shahadah)

The foundation stone of Islam is the formula known as the *Shahadah* (the Creed, or Testimony of Faith), which states, *La ilaha illa-'llah, Muhammadun rasulu 'llah* ('There is no god but God, Muhammad is the Messenger of God'). The first part of the formula consists of a negation and an affirmation. *La ilaha* is the negation of everything, whether it exists in the outer or inner world; *illa-'llah* is the affirmation that only God truly exists. Everything that appears 'other than He' is non-existent. The formula is such that it can be used with any one of the Most Beautiful Names (the Attributes or Qualities of

God) – for example, 'there is no truth but the Truth', 'there is no reality but the Real'. It can also be applied to ourselves, as the negation of the ego or individual self and the affirmation of the Spirit of God within us, 'there is no self but the Self'. The realization of this negation and affirmation, where the individual self is concerned, is expressed in the culminating stages of the Sufi Path as 'self-annihilation' or 'passing away' (*fana'*) and 'subsistence' (*baqa'*) (*see* page 88).

In the *Mathnawi*, Rumi links the *shahadah* with a verse from the Qur'an that expresses the same principle of negation and affirmation, *There is no god but He. Everything perishes, except His Face* (Q 28:88).

> *Everything perishes, except His Face*: Unless you are in His Face, do not seek to exist.
> *Everything perishes* no longer applies to the one who has passed away in Our Face,
> because he is in *but God*, he has gone beyond *no god*; whoever is in *but God* has not passed away.
> Whoever is saying 'I' and 'we' at the door, has turned his back on the door and remains in *no god*.

(M I: 3052–5)

In another verse from the *Mathnawi*, we are reminded that once the self has passed away, only subsistence in God remains.

> He said *There is no god*, then He said *but God: There is no god* became *but God*, and Oneness blossomed forth.

(M VI: 2266)

Prayer (Salat)

The obligatory prayers are performed five times a day at certain prescribed times, and on Friday – the day of gathering – Muslims assemble in the main mosque of a town to say noon prayers together. Although prayers are recited facing in the 'direction of prayer' (*qiblah*), the Kaaba in Mecca, this means more than simply pointing oneself physically in a particular direction. It also refers to our inner orientation, whether our prayers are said facing our ego or facing God. From a certain point of view, however, there is no separation between what we refer to as 'inner' and 'outer'. Our outer life corresponds to our inner state. For this reason the obligatory prayers instigated by the Prophet involve the physical act of bowing down, an outer gesture that both confirms and helps to develop the inner orientation. But it is more than this, as Rumi explains in the conclusion to the story he tells in *Fihi mafihi* about his father, Baha'uddin Walad (for the first part of the story, *see* page 35).

> Whoever turns his back on the Light of God to face the prayer-niche has assuredly turned his back on the *qiblah*, since the Light of God is the soul of the *qiblah*. People turn to face the Kaaba because it is the direction of prayer appointed by the Prophet. How much more appropriate that He be the direction of prayer, since it was for His sake that the Kaaba was designated as the *qiblah*.
>
> (F 3: A24–5/T13–14)

In *Fihi mafihi*, Rumi is asked the question, 'Is there any way to approach God other than the ritual prayers?'

> The answer is more prayer. But prayer is not confined to outward form alone. That is just the 'shell' of prayer. Ritual prayers have a beginning and an end, and anything that has a beginning and an end is a 'shell'. The words *Allahu akbar* [God is Great] are the beginning of the ritual prayer and *as-salamu alaykum wa rahmatu Llah* [God's peace and blessings be upon you] is its end. Likewise, there is more to the *shahadah* [the Creed or profession of faith] than the formula spoken by the tongue, for it too has a beginning and an end. Everything that can be expressed in words and speech and has a beginning and an end is a 'form', a 'shell'; its 'soul', however, is unrestricted and infinite, and has neither beginning nor end. Furthermore, ritual prayers

were formulated by the prophets. Now, the Prophet Muhammad, who gave the prayer of Muslims its form, said, 'I have a time with God wherein there is room for neither any prophet sent by God, nor any angel near to God in station.' We thus know that the 'soul' of prayer is not this external form alone. Rather it is a state of total absorption, of unconsciousness, which excludes these outward forms. In that state there is not even room for Gabriel, who is pure spirit.

(F 3: A24/T12–13)

Professor Nicholson's translation of this passage concludes with the following addition:

One may say that the man who prays in this fashion is exempt from all religious obligation, since he is deprived of his reason. Absorption in Divine Unity is the soul of prayer.

(Nicholson, *Rumi: Poet and Mystic*, p. 92)

In response to a questioner who asked what is superior to prayer, Rumi returns to the subject of ritual prayer in a later discourse.

One answer is, as I have already said, that the 'soul' of prayer is better than prayer, and this I explained. A second answer is that faith is better than the ritual prayer, for prayer is obligatory five times a day, whereas faith is continuous. Ritual prayer can be neglected if there is a valid excuse, and it may also be postponed under certain circumstances. This is another superiority of faith over prayer, for faith cannot be neglected for any excuse, nor are there any circumstances under which it may be postponed. Faith without prayer is beneficial, whereas there is no benefit in prayer without faith, as is the case with the prayer of hypocrites. Furthermore, ritual prayer differs from one religion to the next, whereas faith does not

change at all; its inner states, its orientation, and so forth
are immutable.

(F 8: A43/T33)

Rumi illustrates the relationship between faith and prayer with a story
about a man who called out the Name of God in his prayers, but
received no reply. The story depends on a verse in the Qur'an, in
which God says, *Call Me, and I shall answer* (Q 40:60).

> One night a certain man called out 'Allah!' until his lips grew
> sweet from the mention of His Name. 'Tell me, O babbler,'
> said the Devil, 'where is the response "I am here" to all this
> calling on God's name? Not a single whisper has come from
> the Throne: how much longer will you call out "Allah" in
> vain?'
>
> Broken-hearted, the man lay down to sleep. In a
> dream he saw Khidr, the green man, [see page 131] who
> spoke to him, saying, 'You have stopped praising God.
> Why have you changed your mind about calling on Him?'
>
> The man replied, 'There was no "I am here" in reply,
> and so I was afraid I had been turned away from the Door.'
>
> 'Not at all,' said Khidr. 'God says, "That 'Allah' of
> yours is My call 'I am here'. The ardour with which you pray
> is My message to you. All your strivings to draw near to Me
> are My way of releasing your bonds and drawing you to
> Me. Your love and fear are the noose to entrap My favour.
> Every 'O Lord' of yours is answered with many an 'I am
> here'."'

(M III: 189–97)

The story parodies the sort of inner dialogue experienced by many as
we travel along the Path, for the 'Devil' in the story personifies the
mental chatter of the rational mind which frequently informs us of the
futility of praying to something that is beyond its grasp. In this respect,
our lack of faith stems from our perceived separation from God. Khidr,

on the other hand, expresses the normally unspoken response that comes from deep within our soul and which emanates from the Unseen. In Book II of the *Mathnawi*, Rumi applies the ending of this anecdotal story to himself.

> Even were I to talk and tell stories until the Day of Resurrection, it is not in my power to describe the spiritual resurrection. The things I say are really an 'O Lord'; the words are the lure for a response from those sweet lips. Why, I ask you, would one fail to pray? Why should one be silent when 'I am here' comes in response to one's 'O Lord'? It is a 'Here I am' that cannot be heard, but it can be tasted and felt in every atom of the body.

> (M II: 1188–91)

The extent to which prayer permeated every atom of Rumi's body is reflected in an ode from the *Divan*, in which he says,

> I have prayed so much that I have become a living
>   prayer –
> Everyone who meets me begs a prayer from me.

> (D 903; Mabey, *Rumi: A Spiritual Treasury*, p. 121)

Fasting (Sawm)

A *hadith* attributed to the Prophet, stresses the importance of fasting: 'The true believer resembles a lute whose voice will not improve unless its belly is empty.' For Muslims, the month of Ramadan, the ninth month of the Muslim calendar, is the month of obligatory fasting, during which one is required to abstain between dawn and sunset from all intake of food and drink as well as smoking and sexual activity. But the fast can be extended beyond these obligatory requirements to include abstention from anything that might stimulate the outer senses of sight, sound, smell, touch and taste: violent images, strident sounds, gossip or slander, obnoxious or sweet smells, and so on. It can even be extended to include the inner faculties, such as thought, memory, emotions and imagination, suggested in an ode to fasting in the *Divan*. The imagery of Rumi's opening lines alludes to the Prophet's *hadith* on fasting as well as to the *Song of the Reed*, the first verses of the *Mathnawi* (*see* page 181).

> What hidden sweetness is to be found in an empty belly!
> We are like lutes – no more, no less.
>   If the lute's belly is full, it cannot lament.
> If your brain and belly are burning from fasting,
>   the fire will cause a constant lament to arise from
>   your breast . . .
> Keep your belly empty,
>   and lament with yearning like the reed-flute.
> Keep your belly empty,
>   and tell of hidden mysteries like the reed-pen.

(D 1739: A2:217)

In other words: fast in this world, eat in the next. Rumi illustrates this principle with a story in *Fihi mafihi*, in which he tells of a dervish who ate some food given him by a beautiful young woman representing, in the context of the story, the attractions of the phenomenal world. As the story reveals, the 'food' the young woman gave to the dervish fed his lower or carnal self (*see* page 198). Ultimately, 'food' refers to anything ingested from the world of form. The more we fill ourselves with images, sensations and thoughts from the phenomenal world, the greater the spiritual distance we place between ourselves and God. Abstaining from the things of this world reduces this distance, demolishes the wall of separation brick by brick. In another ode from the *Divan*, Rumi spells out the reason for fasting:

> Through fasting we sacrifice ourselves for the life of our
>   soul.
> Let's sacrifice the whole body, since the soul is its guest!

(D 892: A1:115)

Alms-giving (Zakat)

The Qur'an stipulates that all Muslims practise regular charity, and that those whose wealth exceeds a certain threshold are under obligation to give a portion of their wealth – in goods or money – annually to the poor. The root from which the word *zakat* is derived means 'to purify' and 'to increase', so the obligation to give alms also has an inner purifying function. It not only 'purifies' the donor's wealth, it also encourages a charitable, generous disposition, and a non-attachment to worldly possessions.

As Annmarie Schimmel, the author of numerous books on Rumi and Islam, points out, *zakat* 'does not much lend itself to poetic elaboration, but Maulana [Rumi], like other Persian poets, sometimes alludes to the *zakat-i la'l*, the tax paid on rubies. As the mouth of the beloved is often compared to a ruby, the *zakat-i la'l* means, in poetical parlance, a kiss that the lover wants to collect from his beloved.' (Schimmel, *Rumi's World*, pp. 146–7) In at least one ode from the *Divan*, Rumi is quite specific, for he says: 'The ruby is the alms of our Beloved' (D122: A1:15).

An example of Rumi's practical teaching on alms-giving is illustrated by an incident recounted by Aflaki, which, according to the author, was relayed to him by Sultan Walad, Rumi's son. One day, two law students came to visit Rumi. They offered him the gift of a few lentils, pleading poverty as an excuse for the meagreness of their donation. Thereupon Rumi narrated the following anecdote involving the Prophet Muhammad.

> God revealed to Mustafa (Muhammad) that the believers should contribute of their possessions, for the service of God, as much as they could spare. Some brought the half, some the third part; Abu Bakr brought the whole of what he possessed. Thus a large treasure was collected, of money, animals, and arms, for God's service.
>
> A poor woman, too, brought three dates and a loaf of bread, which were all she had on earth. The disciples smiled. Mustafa perceived their action, and said that God

had showed him a vision, which he wished to tell them.

'God has removed the veil from my eyes, and I saw that the angels had placed together in one dish of a scale the whole of your very liberal offerings, and in the other dish the three dates and one loaf of this poor woman. The contents of the latter dish outweighed all the rest.'

The disciples bowed, thanked the Prophet, and asked him to explain the inner meaning of his vision. He replied, 'This poor woman has parted with her all, whereas my disciples have kept back a part of their possessions. As the proverbs say, "The generous one is generous out of what he possesses," and "A little, in the eyes of the Most Great, is much." You bury a single date-stone in the ground, entrusting it to God. He makes that stone become a tree, which yields much fruit, because the stone was entrusted to Him. Therefore, let your alms be given to the poor, and to God's servants, and entrust them to God. For it is said, "Alms fall first into God's hand, before reaching the hands of the poor".'

(Aflaki, *Legends of the Sufis*, pp. 69–70)

Pilgrimage (Hajj)

As we have seen, the sacred precinct at Mecca had been a place of pilgrimage in pre-Islamic times, and part of the annual pilgrimage entailed the circumambulation of the Kaaba. The Prophet Muhammad destroyed the pagan idols in the Kaaba when he took the city of Mecca in 630, and he performed the first full Islamic pilgrimage in 632, the year in which he died. It is incumbent upon Muslims, but not obligatory, to undertake the pilgrimage to Mecca at least once in their lifetime.

The pilgrimage to Mecca can be understood in terms of a conscious journey towards the Source of our being. As with the physical *hajj*, it is incumbent upon us to make this spiritual journey but it is not obligatory, for as the Qur'an says, *There shall be no compulsion in religion* (Q 2:256). The nature of the journey to the Source of our being is such that we need only make it once in our lifetime. For as Rumi makes clear, it is a journey of self-realization, a journey that begins and ends within us.

> O pilgrims on the path, where are you?
> Here is the Beloved! Here!
> Your beloved is your neighbour,
> just the other side of the wall.
> Why do you err in the desert?
> If you look at the Beloved's Face,
> and don't fix your gaze on form,
> you become the House, and its lord,
> for you are the Kaaba! You!

(D 648, after Lewis, *Rumi*, pp. 384–5)

Chapter Four

Rumi and the Sufi Path

The Sufi is the child of the present moment, my friend.
The word 'tomorrow' is excluded from the doctrine of
those who travel the Path.

(M I: 123)

Although Rumi is renowned as a Sufi saint and one of the foremost
exponents of the Sufi Path, his principal teaching works – the
Mathnawi and *Fihi mafihi* – do not offer an overtly explicit description
of the Sufi Path and practices. Even while it was still being written, the
Mathnawi was criticised by those who were looking for a more readily
recognizable treatise on the Sufi Path or a scholarly exposition of
profound esoteric truths. Rumi included his response to one such
critic towards the end of Book III of the *Mathnawi* (for an extended
version of this response, *see* page 201.)

> Even before this story reaches its conclusion, the foul
> stench of envy wafts in my direction . . . All of a sudden, an
> ass sticks his head out of his stable and, braying like an old
> crone, says, 'This work' (he means the *Mathnawi*) 'is poor,
> the story of the Prophet retold, nothing more. It has no
> discussion of those profound mysteries towards which the
> saints gallop in haste, nor of the stations from asceticism to
> self-effacement which lead step by step to union with God.
> It lacks any explanation of the stages and stations, those
> wings by which the mystic soars on high.'
>
> O critical dog! You are doing a lot of noisome barking
> . . . But I will follow the advice of the Sage of Ghazna: I will
> not allow myself to be affected by these taunts . . . Does a

caravan ever turn back from a journey because of the barking of dogs?

(M III: 4227, 4232–6, 4282, 4291; M VI: 12)

Rumi's critic appears to have been more concerned with the form of the *Mathnawi* than its essence. For readers unfamiliar with the history of the Sufis and the principles underlying the Sufi Path to enlightenment, the first part of this chapter offers a brief overview of these two aspects of Sufism.

THE SUFIS FROM MUHAMMAD TO RUMI

The seventh century and the first Sufis
One of the first treatises on Sufism, *Kashf al-Mahjub* (Revelation of the Veiled), was written in the eleventh century by al-Hujwiri, a Sufi from Ghazna, the capital and cultural centre of the Ghaznavid Empire founded by Sultan Mahmud (*see* 'The Islamic World', page 24). In his treatise, Hujwiri quotes the following words of the tenth-century Sufi, Abu 'l-Hasan Fushanji, 'Today Sufism (*tasawwuf*) is a name without a reality, but formerly it was a reality without a name.' Hujwiri continues, 'In the time of the Companions of the Prophet and their immediate successors this name did not exist, but its reality was in everyone. Now the name exists, but not the reality' (*Kashf al-Mahjub*, p. 44). Hujwiri's assertion that 'the reality of *tasawwuf* was in everyone' is significant. For effectively it infers that not only were the Prophet and his Companions the first Muslims, they were also mystics, and the first Sufis in all but name.

The Sufis and the 'ulama'
With the passing of the Prophet Muhammad and the four 'Rightly-Guided' caliphs, there was a partial return to pre-Islamic ways, at least among those who had embraced Islam for the sake of expediency or to benefit from the spoils of war. There was also disagreement over the rightful leadership of the community. Although the Caliph was

nominally the spiritual leader of Islam, the three aspects of authority that had been united in the Prophet – the legal, theological and mystical – now became divided between the jurists, the theologians and the mystics. Essentially, these three fell into two camps – the jurists and theologians, and the mystics – which reflected the exoteric and esoteric aspects of Islam. The two camps were guided respectively by the *'ulama'* (the religious authorities) and the Sufi shaykhs. Without the strong presence of the latter, the *'ulama'* would have gained unique control of the Islamic tradition and imposed their legalistic and religious authority in whatever way they saw fit. They might even have created an overall religious authority for the Islamic community, similar to that of the Vatican for Western Christianity prior to the Protestant Reformation.

In brief, the *'ulama'* concerned themselves with the outer law (*shari'ah*) while the Sufis tended the inner path (*tariqah*), the 'mystical heart of Islam', guiding the development of the religion (and the Islamic community) from within. This was a spiritual duty that the Sufis could not (and still cannot) avoid, but the way in which they manifested their guidance differed according to circumstances. Whereas exoteric religious, political and social authorities tend to create monolithic structures that need an ever-increasing number of laws to maintain some semblance of stability, Sufis are not attached to outward form. It is the *essence* which is important.

The eighth century

By the time the celebrated woman Sufi saint Rabi'ah al-'Adawiyyah of Basra was born in around 717, less than a hundred years after the death of the Prophet, the spiritual climate of the Islamic world had undergone a dramatic change. Rabi'ah was born at a time when the power of the Ummayad dynasty was at its height, and its territory comprised the largest empire the world had ever seen. Territorial expansion coincided with a decline in spiritual awareness. Against this background, Rabi'ah spoke out more boldly than her predecessors, urging people to surrender themselves to God with a directness that knew no compromise. She was also one of the first Sufis to give ecstatic voice to the theme of Divine Love, a theme that was later to find its highest form of expression in the writings of Rumi and other Persian poets of the twelfth and thirteenth centuries. The Sufis of the eighth century were also renowned for their humility and asceticism, perhaps none more so than the Prince of Balkh, Ibrahim ibn Adham, to whom we shall return later (*see* page 99).

The ninth and tenth centuries

The conquest of new lands in the seventh and eighth centuries brought with it an influx of converts to Islam, many of whom brought with them elements of other religious beliefs and traditions. Some attempts were made to graft these on to Islam, resulting in several heresies that were subsequently dealt with by the religious authorities. Having become more powerful in the second half of the eighth century under the 'Abbasid rulers, the *'ulama'* were on their guard against further heresies and they eyed the Sufis with suspicion. Things came to a head in the ninth century with the emergence of what is often referred to as the 'intoxicated school' of Sufism, also known as the 'drunken', 'inebriated' or 'ecstatic' Sufis. Yet this is not so much a 'school' in the conventional sense but a term used to refer to those Sufis, such as Bayazid al-Bistami (*see* page 101), who, in moments of ecstatic union with the Divine, delivered inspired utterances that could be taken as blasphemous. For the exoteric *'ulama'*, the 'ecstatic' Sufis were heretics. None more so than al-Hallaj (*see* page 102) who was tried, condemned for blasphemy and executed in 922 in Baghdad, the Abbasid capital.

The eleventh century

The tenth and eleventh centuries saw a proliferation of textbooks and treatises by Sufis, many of which were written with the intention of avoiding further misunderstanding and confrontation with the religious authorities. Hujwiri's *Kashf al-Mahjub* is an example of the treatises that were written at this time. The figure who may have done more than anyone else to bridge the divide between orthodox Islam and the Sufis was Abu Hamid al-Ghazali (d. 1111). Ghazali was teaching in one of the most important theological colleges in Baghdad when he experienced a profound spiritual crisis. Theology alone was unable to resolve this crisis, so he withdrew from teaching and lived the life of an ascetic. He wandered the land in search of the Truth for the next ten years, during which time he encountered the Sufis, whose teachings and practices helped to resolve his crisis. Ghazali eventually resumed his teaching post, and the high regard in which he is held by Muslims, as well as the considerable influence of his writings, served to reposition Sufism in its rightful place as a continuation of the original mystical heart of Islam.

The twelfth and thirteenth centuries

With justifiable reason, the twelfth and thirteenth centuries are considered to have been the Golden Age of Sufism. It was an age that began with Ghazali (d. 1111) and the integration of Sufi principles at the heart of Islam; it gave birth to the great Sufi Orders of the Qadiri, Chishti, Shadhili, Mevlevi and others; it was the age of the great Sufi masters Jalaluddin Rumi and Muhyiddin Ibn 'Arabi (d. 1240), whose continuing influence extends beyond Islam and Sufism into the wider world. It was also a time that witnessed the flowering of Persian poetry. Arabic was the language of the Qur'an and the first language of Islam, but from the twelfth to the fifteenth centuries there was a flowering of Persian poetry as a vehicle for expounding Sufi teaching. Until Rumi's poetry reached a Western audience in the twentieth century, the most widely known work of Persian Sufi poetry was probably the *Rubba'iyyat* (a collection of quatrains) of Omar Khayyam, thanks to Edward Fitzgerald's nineteenth-century English translation. Hakim Sana'i of Ghazna (d.c. 1150), to whom Rumi refers as 'the sage of Ghazna', is considered to have broken new ground by using the traditional *mathnawi* (couplet) for spiritual instruction in his *Hadiqat al-haqiqah* (Garden of the Truth). Another great Persian Sufi poet of this period with whose work Rumi was familiar is Fariduddin Attar (1142–1220/1229), famous for his *Mantiq al-tair* (Conference of the Birds).

The Sufi Orders

The Sufi Orders, which began to appear in the tenth century, are not to be confused with the monastic orders of Christianity. The latter are closed or semi-closed monastic orders, whereas the Arabic word translated into English as 'Order' is *tariqah*, which we encountered earlier in the context of its alternative meaning of the inner or spiritual path. The Sufi Orders are more in the nature of brotherhoods that gather around a shaykh or spiritual master. When the Prophet was alive, his close followers had sat around him to receive his teaching. Because this was part of the Prophetic Sunnah, the same system was adopted by later generations of Muslims. The Sufi *tariqahs* arose naturally when a group of followers began to gather around a particular shaykh; with the passing of time the group came to be known by the name of the shaykh whose teaching it followed. For example, the *tariqah* that formed around Shaykh Abd al-Qadir al-Jilani (d.1166) in Baghdad became known as the *Qadiriyyah* or Qadiri Order. Likewise, Rumi's followers became known as the *Mevleviyyah* or Mevlevi, after Rumi's honorific title of *Mevlana* (Our Master). Each Sufi Order has its own initiatic chain of transmission – the *silsilah* – which connects the shaykhs of today with the first Sufi shaykh, the Prophet Muhammad. Sufi Orders are now active in all parts of the world, although some are active on some continents but not on others. In some Orders, women and men enjoy equal status.

THE SUFI PATH

Stages of the Path

The Sufi is one who acknowledges that he or she has no alternative but to seek union with the Beloved, for every atom of their body yearns to be reunited with the Source of its being. The particular stages of the path were fully defined in the early treatises on Sufism – such as Hujwiri's *Kashf al-Mahjub*. An even earlier treatise, the *Kitab al-Luma* defines the seven stages as: repentance, abstinence, renunciation, poverty, patience, trust in God and satisfaction (Nicholson, *Mystics of Islam*, p. 29). One of the best-known and most accessible expositions of the Path – and what each stage entails – is Attar's *Conference of the Birds* in which the seven stages are depicted as seven valleys through which the seeker has to pass in order to attain union with the Beloved. Attar's seven valleys are: the quest, love, understanding, detachment, unity, astonishment, and poverty and annihilation. Although the path to the Beloved is frequently described as comprising the above seven stages, some Sufis say there are only two stages: dying to the self, and union with the Divine.

The nafs

The Arabic word *nafs* is variously translated as 'soul', 'self' or 'ego'. The *nafs* has seven levels or stages of development that correspond more or less to the seven stages of the Sufi Path. The Path, which leads to a transformation of consciousness, can therefore be described as the refinement and purification of the soul. The seven *nafs* are generally defined as:

- *nafs al-ammara* – the commanding or compulsive-obsessive self, also known as the carnal or animal self, is entirely governed by its desires, passions and instincts.
- *nafs al-lawwama* – the accusing or blaming self, corresponds to the awakening of conscience and a realization of the extent to which one's actions are controlled by the *nafs al-ammara*.
- *nafs al-mulhama* – the inspired or balanced self marks the beginning of genuine spiritual integration and a release of the self from the tyranny of physical instincts and the desires of the ego.
- *nafs al-mutma'inna* – the tranquil self or self at peace, as its name implies, has attained a degree of detachment from worldly concerns and an increasing awareness of the Presence of God in all things.
- *nafs al-radiyya* – the fulfilled or satisfied self is the initial merging or union of the individual with God.
- *nafs al-mardiyya* – the fulfilling or satisfying self, also described as the self of total submission, is the merging of God with the individual.

• *nafs al-kamila* – the perfected and complete self is the state of total union with God and the attainment of universal consciousness.

Of the nafs al- ammara, Rumi says:

> Your *nafs* is the mother of all idols: a material idol is only
>   a snake, but the idol of the *nafs* is a dragon . . .
> Breaking a material idol is easy, very easy; to regard the
>   *nafs* as easy to subdue is folly, folly.
> O son, if you want to know the form of the *nafs*, read the
>   description of the seven gates of hell!

>   (M I: 772, 778–9)

> The *nafs* has the name of God on its lips and the Qur'an
>   in its hand, but up its sleeve it has a dagger.

>   (M III: 2554)

> When the *nafs* says 'meow' like the cat,
> I put it in the bag like the cat!

>   (D 1656: Schimmel, *Rumi's World*, p. 106)

> Wield the mace against yourself and smash your ego to pieces, for
> the carnal eye is like an ear stuffed with cotton wool.

>   (M VI: 732)

Fana' *and* baqa'

Fana' is the passing away or effacement of the self. The final stage of *fana'* is *fana' al-fana'* (the passing-away of passing-away, or the effacement of effacement), in which one is no longer conscious of having attained *fana'*.

Baqa', which is from the same root as *al-Baqi*, one of the Ninety-Nine Names of God, refers to the Divine Attribute of Everlastingness or Continuance. As such, it is the opposite of *fana'*. Both terms are met in a verse in the Qur'an: *Everything upon the earth shall pass away; but the Face of the Lord shall remain forever . . .* (Q 55:26–7). That which passes away is impermanent, transient. That which remains is permanent, enduring. The principle of *fana'* or 'dying to self' is implicit in the *hadith* 'Die before you die' (*see* page 90). As Rumi explains, when Sufis attain the stage of *fana'* and leaves their transient self behind, that which remains is the enduring Presence of God.

> The seeker of God's Court is like this: when God appears, the seeker disappears.
> For although union with God brings immortality, the attainment of undying life [*baqa'*] means first dying to your self [*fana'*].
> The shadows that seek the Light are like this: when the Light shines, the shadows disappear.
> Can reason remain alive when consumed by His Light? *Everything that exists will perish except His Face* [Q 28:88].
> Existence and non-existence perish before His Face: what a miracle, to exist in non-existence!
>
> (M III: 4658–62)

> It is said, 'There is no dervish in the world; or, if there is a dervish, he doesn't really exist.' What exists is his spiritual essence; his human attributes have passed away in the Divine Attributes. He is like a candle flame in full sunlight: the light of the flame is barely visible, yet reason tells us it exists.
>
> (M III: 3671–2)

> At night people light a lamp in the house so that its light may spare the occupants from darkness. The lamp is like the human body, whose light is the carnal soul. Lamps need wicks and oil. So does the body. The physical senses are the body's wicks, its oil is food and sleep. Without food and sleep the body doesn't live for long, but then it doesn't live

for long even with food and sleep. The body cannot last without wicks and oil, nor does it last with wicks and oil, since the body's light stems from other causes. It is inevitable that its light is extinguished: how can it persist when it is annihilated by the full light of the sun? Similarly, all human faculties are non-lasting, reduced to nothing on the Day of Resurrection. Yet the light of the senses and spirit of our fathers does not perish completely, like the grass. But, like the light of the moon and the stars, they all vanish in the sun's radiance . . .

Those who have forsaken the world do not cease to exist, for they are suffused with the Divine Attributes. All their personal attributes have been effaced in the Attributes of God, just as a star vanishes without trace in the presence of the sun. If you require evidence from the Qur'an for this, recite, *All of them shall be brought into Our Presence* [Q 36:32 and 53]. The person who is brought into the Presence is not non-existent. If you understand this, you may gain a sure knowledge of the everlasting life [*baqa'*] of the spirit. The spirit excluded from everlasting life lives in torment; the spirit that unites with God and attains everlasting life is free from all limitations.

(M IV: 425–33, 442–6)

'Die before you die'

This *hadith*, which encapsulates the purpose and goal of the Sufi Path, is illustrated by Rumi's story of the student and the shroud.

THE STUDENT AND THE SHROUD

An ounce of Divine favour is better than all the contrivances of the human mind. So, give up all your cunning machinations, because nothing happens until you die to the schemings of the human mind. Listen to the story of Sadri Jahan.

Sadri Jahan of Bukhara was exceedingly generous to those in need. It was his custom to wrap gold coins in bits of paper and distribute them as freely as the sun and moon radiate their light. Every morning Jahan distributed alms to a different set of people, so that none felt left out. One day he would give to the sick, the next to widows, students of religious law, impoverished townsfolk, debtors, and so on, each group in turn. However, it was a rule of his that he never gave alms to any one who asked for them verbally. The people who were to receive alms would stand in silence, lining his path. But, if any one so much as opened their lips, they were punished by being given no alms. Jahan's motto was, 'Blessed are the silent', and it was for those who remained silent that he reserved his gifts of food and money.

Now it so happened that one day an old man blurted out, 'Give me alms, I'm starving.'

Jahan refused to give him any alms. But, to everyone's astonishment, the old man persisted. 'You shameless old man,' said Jahan.

Quick as a flash, the old man retorted, 'You're more shameless than me, for you enjoy this world and you are so greedy that you hope your generosity will bring you enjoyment in the next world as well.'

When he heard this reply, Jahan laughed, and, making an exception to his strict rule of giving only to those who were silent, gave alms to the old man.

A few days later it was the turn of the law students to receive alms. On this occasion one of the law students began to whine as Jahan drew near to him. Jahan heard him, and punished the student by giving him nothing. The next day it was the turn of the sick, and the student tied both his legs up in splints and stood in line, head lowered in the hope that he would not be recognised. But Jahan recognized the student, and again gave him nothing. The next day the student concealed his face under a hood and stood in line with the impoverished townsfolk, but Jahan still recognized him. The student tried all sorts of trickery. On one occasion he even donned a *chadar* and stood with the women; on another he sat, head down, with the widows, but to no avail.

The student became so desperate that in the end he went to a shroudmaker, saying, 'Wrap me in a shroud and lay me out on the road. Don't say a word, but sit and watch until Sadri Jahan passes by. Perhaps he will see me and, thinking I'm dead, will give alms to pay for the shroud. Whatever he gives, I'll split it fifty-fifty with you.'

The shroudmaker did exactly as he had been told, and wrapped the student in a shroud and laid him out on the road. When Sadri Jahan passed by he dropped some gold coins on the shroud. A hand immediately shot out from under the shroud and grabbed the coins, for the student was afraid that the shroudmaker would take the gold and keep it for himself. Sticking his head out of the shroud, the student said to Jahan, 'You refused to give me alms, but I found a way of getting them in the end!'

'Ah, you stubborn man,' replied Jahan. 'But you had to die first!'

This is the meaning of 'Die before you die'. The rewards come after you die, not before. You can scheme all you like, but dying is the only means of attaining Divine favour. And a single Divine favour is better than any kind of personal effort, for personal effort can entail all sorts of trickery. To receive the Divine favour you need to die first. Those who know have tried and tested this method: receipt of the Divine favour is not possible without the mystical death. So, don't hang about. Don't even hesitate where Divine favour is concerned!

(M VI: 3798–842)

Die now, die now, die in Love;
when you have died in Love,
you will all be given new life.

(D 636)

Death calls on humanity
myriad times every day;
the lover of God slays himself,
he doesn't wait to be called.

(D 728; A1:90)

Tales of the Sufi Path

THE CHICKPEA AND THE COOKING-POT

Look at the chickpea in the pot, and how it leaps to the surface as the heat is turned up. When the chickpea is being cooked it keeps bobbing to the top of the pot, complaining, 'Why are you doing this to me? You bought me, so why are you making me suffer?'

Every time it bobs to the surface, the cook knocks the chickpea back down firmly with her ladle, saying, 'No! Don't jump out! Give in to the cooking and stop trying to escape from the heat. I'm not boiling you out of spite, but so that you become full of flavour and nutritious, and able to blend with the vital essence of human beings. Such suffering does not diminish you. When you were young and fresh, you drank rainwater in the garden. That drinking was for this heat.'

God's mercy comes before His wrath, so that through His mercy you may experience the suffering of existence. Without life's pleasures, the fleshly self would not grow. And if the self didn't grow, what food would there be for Divine Love to consume? You experience the suffering of existence so that you may become non-existent. When your suffering is over, God's mercy will justify your ordeal, saying, 'Now you have been purified [of the self], you have left the river of suffering.'

'Oh, chickpea,' says the housewife, 'You drank your fill in the springtime, now you are host to pain and suffering: treat your guests well! . . . Carry on cooking, until all traces of existence and self have been boiled away. You enjoyed yourself in the worldly garden, but in reality you are a rose in the spiritual garden. If you have been torn from the garden of water and clay, it is so that you may become food for human mouths and enter the chain of life. Become food, energy, and thoughts! . . .'

'Oh woman,' said the chickpea, 'if that's the case, help me to cook some more! Since you're the cook, hit me with your ladle, for I love your blows. I'm like an elephant that needs beating so it won't dream of being back in the gardens of Hindustan. Hit me until I surrender myself to the boiling so that I may find a way to the Beloved. When human beings are in a state of separation, they grow wilful and contrary, like the dreaming elephant. When the elephant dreams of Hindustan, he ignores his driver and becomes obtuse.'

'I used to be like you, a child of clay,' said the cook. 'But after a lengthy period of self-mortification I became acceptable food. First I was cooked in the world, then I was cooked in the body. These two cookings empowered the senses and developed the self, and then I became your teacher. I used to say to myself, "All this churning is so that you may become clothed with knowledge and spiritual attributes." Having become self, further cooking will take me beyond self.'

(M III: 4159–71, 4178–81, 4197–4208)

THE GREEK AND CHINESE PAINTERS

If you desire to pass beyond the outer form of things, free yourself totally from your lower self . . . Cleanse yourself of its attributes so that you may see your own pure and untarnished essence, and perceive in your heart the knowledge of the prophets, without book, without teacher, without master . . . And if you wish to hear an allegory about this hidden knowledge, listen to the story of the Greek and Chinese painters.

Some Greek and Chinese painters were once having an argument about the art of painting.

'We are the better artists,' said the Chinese.

'We are the true masters,' replied the Greeks.

'I will give you a test to see whose claim is justified,' said the king.

The two groups began to discuss the matter, but the Greeks withdrew from the debate. So the Chinese suggested they be given two rooms, one for themselves and one for the Greeks. The doors of the rooms they were given faced each other but were closed off by a curtain.

The Chinese asked the king for a hundred different colours, and every morning the royal treasury was opened so that they could be given the precious pigments they had requested. The Greeks declined to use pigments of any kind. They asked instead for polishing materials and, shutting themselves in their room, they polished away at the walls until they became as clear as the open sky.

There is a process that effects a transition from multi-colours to colourlessness: colour can be compared to the clouds, and colourlessness to the moon. Whenever you see wonderful colours lighting up the clouds, know that this comes from the sun, the moon, and the stars.

When the Chinese had finished their work, the king entered their room to look at what they had painted. He was awed by what he saw. Then the Greeks drew aside the curtain that separated the two rooms. The reflection of the Chinese paintings shone back from the highly polished walls. Everything that the king had seen in the other room was even more beautiful than before. So much so that it bedazzled the eyes.

The Greeks are the Sufis, whose knowledge does not come from studying books, as scholars do. Instead they have polished their hearts until they have removed all traces of greed, desire, envy, and hatred. A pure heart is without doubt like a polished mirror, open to receive an infinite number of images . . .

Those who polish their hearts have set themselves free from the attractions of scent and colour: they perceive Beauty directly, at every moment. Abandoning superficial knowledge, they have acquired the eye of certainty. Passing beyond the realm of thought, they have arrived at the Light. They have reached the essence, the ocean of true knowledge. Whilst death strikes fear into the heart of most people, Sufis hold it in contempt. Affliction falls on the shell of the oyster, not on the pearl, therefore nothing has power over their hearts. They have abandoned learning and jurisprudence and taken up self-abandonment and spiritual poverty . . . Such is their state of purity that they receive an infinity of images from the heavens, the stars, and the void, as though God were seeing through their eyes.

(M I: 3458–9, 3460–1, 3466–85, 3492–7, 3499)

The Sufi Shaykh

The Sufi teacher or spiritual guide – known as a *shaykh* (Arabic), or *pir* (Persian) – is held in the highest regard by his followers, and treated with great respect. The reason for this is explained in the following anecdote, which, according to Aflaki, was related by Rumi to his son, Sultan Walad:

A true disciple is he who holds his teacher to be superior to all others. So much so, that, for instance, a disciple of Bayazid Bistami was once asked whether Bayazid or Abu-Hanifa [d. 767, the eponymous founder of the Hanafi school of jurisprudence] was the greater, and he replied that his teacher, Bayazid, was the greater.

'Then,' said the questioner, 'is Bayazid the greater, or is Abu Bakr?'

'My teacher is the greater.'

'Bayazid or Muhammad?'

'Bayazid.'

'Bayazid or God?'

'I only know my teacher, I know no other than him; and I know that he is greater than all the others.'

Another was asked the last question, and he replied,

'There is no difference between the two.'

A third was asked, and he said, 'It would require a greater one than either of the two to determine which of them is the greater.'

As God does not walk in this world of sensible objects, the prophets are the substitute of God. No, no! I am wrong! For if you suppose that those substitutes and their principal are two different things, you have judged erroneously.

(Aflaki, *Legends of the Sufis*, pp. 67–8)

The following incident, which further illustrates the respect accorded the Sufi teacher, also offers a helpful definition of the Sufi terms *faqr* (poverty) and *faqir* or *dervish* (poor one).

One day Rumi paid a visit to a great shaykh. He was received with the greatest respect, and, seated with the shaykh on the same carpet, they both fell into a state of ecstatic spiritual communion.

A certain dervish, who had undertaken the pilgrimage to Mecca many times, was also present. He addressed Rumi, and asked, 'What is poverty?' Rumi did not reply, and so the dervish repeated his question three times.

When Rumi left the gathering, the shaykh accompanied him to the door. On his return to the room, he severely reprimanded the dervish for the way he had intruded on his guest. 'Especially,' said the shaykh, 'as he fully answered your question the first time you asked it.' The bewildered dervish asked the shaykh what Rumi's answer had been.

'The poor man,' said the shaykh, 'when he knows God, is tongue-tied. The real dervish is the one who, when in the presence of saints, remains silent. He says nothing, either with his tongue or with his heart. This is what is meant by *Listen in silence* [Q 46:28].'

(Aflaki, *Legends of the Sufis*, pp. 63–64)

The role of the saint

The role of the saint is illustrated in the following episode related by Aflaki, which is said to have taken place shortly before Rumi's death.

> One day, a company of dervishes and learned men united in extolling the Parvana [the Seljuk vizier of Rum] in Rumi's presence. He endorsed everything they said, and added, 'The Parvana merits your praise a hundredfold. But there is another side to the matter, which may be illustrated by the following anecdote:
>
>> A group of pilgrims were once making their way across the desert towards Mecca, when one of their camels collapsed from exhaustion. Try as they might, the pilgrims could not get the camel to stand up again, so they transferred its load to another beast. The fallen animal was abandoned to its fate, and the caravan resumed its journey.
>>
>> It was not long before the camel was surrounded by a circle of ravenous wild beasts – wolves, jackals, and so on. But none of these beasts ventured to attack him. The members of the caravan became aware of this extraordinary behaviour, and one of them went back to investigate. He found that an amulet had been left hanging from the camel's neck. He removed the amulet, and after he had retreated a short distance the hungry predators fell upon the poor camel and tore him to pieces.
>
> 'Now,' said Rumi, 'this world is in a situation exactly like that of that poor camel. The learned of the world are the company of pilgrims, and our existence among them is the amulet suspended round the neck of the camel, which is the world. As long as we remain suspended, the world will go on, the caravan will proceed. But as soon as the divine

command shall be spoken, *O soul at peace, return to your Lord, pleased and pleasing unto Him* [Q 89:27–8], and we are removed from the neck of the world-camel, people will see how it shall fare with the world – how its inhabitants shall be driven – what shall become of its sultans, its lawyers, its scribes.'

(Aflaki, *Legends of the Sufis*, pp. 33–4)

Three Sufis

IBRAHIM IBN ADHAM

Born in Balkh, in Rumi's home province of Khorasan in eastern Persia, Ibrahim ibn Adham (d.782) is variously described as a prince, king or sultan. In pre-Muslim times, Balkh had been a flourishing Buddhist centre, and the ruins of Buddhist monasteries were still visible there centuries after the arrival of Islam. Attention is frequently drawn to the similarities between the principal events of the life of Ibrahim ibn Adham and that of the Buddha: like the Buddha, Ibrahim was a prince whose search for truth inspired him to renounce his worldly kingdom and earthly possessions and lead the life of a wandering ascetic.

The abundant stories about Ibrahim ibn Adham can be divided loosely into two categories: in one he is portrayed as the model of asceticism and humility; in the other he is subjected to various acts of humiliation to rid him of any last vestiges of this-worldly self. Rumi gives two accounts of Ibrahim ibn Adham's renunciation of the world, the first of which occurred while Ibrahim was out hunting, the second while he was reclining in his palace.

When he was still a king, Ibrahim ibn Adham went out hunting. He galloped off in pursuit of a deer and became totally separated from his soldiers. Although his horse was sweating heavily, he galloped on. When he had ridden beyond the edge of the plain, the deer turned to him and spoke, 'You were not created for this. You did not come from not-being into being in order to hunt me down. Supposing you did catch me, what then?'

On hearing these words, Ibrahim uttered a cry and

flung himself off his horse. There was no one in that wilderness apart from a shepherd, with whom Ibrahim pleaded, saying, 'Take my jewel-encrusted royal garments, my weapons and my horse, and give me your coarse woollen robe. Tell no one of this, nor of what has become of me.' Putting on the woollen robe, he went on his way.

Now, consider what his intention was and the outcome intended by God. Ibrahim's desire was to catch the deer, but the deer was God's means of catching him. So realize that things happen in this world according to His will and purpose.

(F 44: A170/T169)

When Ibrahim exchanged his royal garments for the shepherd's woollen robe, the garment worn by dervishes (literally 'the poor'), he became a Sufi both outwardly and inwardly. In Rumi's closing comment, he draws attention to a traditional Sufi theme: whatever our own intention may be for doing the things we do in this world, our actions are simultaneously an act of free will and an act of God (*see* page 178).

One night when Ibrahim was reclining on his throne, he heard someone shouting and tramping over the roof of his palace. 'Who is that?' he asked himself, and then shouted from the palace window, 'Who goes there? This is not the sound of human footsteps, it must be a jinn.'

The mysterious visitors peered over the edge of the roof, saying, 'We're a search party doing our rounds.'

'What are you searching for?' asked Ibrahim.

'Our camels,' they replied.

'Who ever heard of anyone searching for camels on a rooftop?'

'We are following your example,' came the reply. 'Who ever heard of anyone seeking union with God while reclining on a throne?'

It was no more than that. Ibrahim vanished, and was never seen again. Like the jinn, he became invisible to human eyes. Although he moved among the people, his real self was hidden from them, since what do people see other than the outer garments? When he vanished from the sight of friends and strangers, his fame spread throughout the world, like that of the Anka. For whenever any bird reaches Mount Qaf, the whole world proclaims the good news.

(M IV: 829–38)

The last sentence alludes to Fariduddin Attar's, *The Conference of the Birds*, an allegory of the Sufi Path, in which a group of birds attain union with God by making the arduous journey to Mount Qaf, a mythical mountain that lies beyond the limits of the known world. The Anka was an Arabian bird, similar to the Phoenix, but of huge size.

BAYAZID AL-BISTAMI

Born in Bistam in north-eastern Persia, Bayazid al-Bistami (d. 875/7) is widely acknowledged as the first of the so-called 'ecstatic' or 'drunken' Sufis, who were famous (even infamous) for the sayings they uttered while in an ecstatic state of union with God. Some of these sayings were considered blasphemous by the religious authorities. Where stories about Ibrahim ibn Adham cite him as the model of humility, those about Bistami generally concern themselves with the state of *fana'*.

Bistami's most famous ecstatic saying occurred in the conversation that took place at the first meeting of Rumi and Shams of Tabriz, 'Glory be to me! How great is My Majesty!' (*see* page 38). In the *Mathnawi*, Rumi relates what happened when Bistami made the original declaration to his disciples. The following is an abridged prose version of Rumi's account.

> That esteemed dervish, Bayazid Bistami, went to his disciples and said, 'I am God! There is no God but me, so worship me!'
> The next morning, when his ecstatic state had passed, his disciples told him that he had blasphemed. 'If I do it

again,' said Bayazid, 'take up your knives and stab me. God is beyond the body, and I am in the body, so kill me if I ever say anything like that again.'

This instruction to his disciples vanished from his mind when Bayazid next entered a state of ecstasy. He spoke more strongly than before, saying, 'Under my cloak there is nothing but God. Why are you looking for Him elsewhere?'

At this, his disciples took up their knives and began to stab him. But each time they plunged their knives into their Shaykh, they cut themselves. The Master remained unscathed while his disciples bled. Whoever slashed at Bayazid's throat ended up cutting his own. Whoever stabbed at his heart pierced his own breast and died. Those who knew and respected that spiritual colossus struck half-heartedly at him and only wounded themselves slightly. Their half-knowledge saved them from certain death.

When dawn broke, only a few disciples were left. The moans that came from the house attracted a large crowd. One of the crowd said to Bayazid, 'You, who contain the two worlds in a single cloak, if your body were human it would have been slain by those knives.'

Those who stab at a self-less person with a knife are stabbing themselves. Be warned! The self-less one has passed away in God and he is safe because there is no self to harm. His form has passed away and he has become a mirror in which nothing is seen but the reflection of another. If you spit at it, you spit in your own face; if you strike it, you hit yourself. If you see an ugly face in the mirror, it's you. If you see Jesus and Mary in it, this too is you. Self-less and without form, the one who has passed away is neither this nor that. He is a mirror in which all we see is the image of ourselves.

(M IV: 2102–43)

MANSUR AL-HALLĀJ

The son of a wool or cotton-carder (Arabic *hallāj*), Mansur al-Hallāj was born in 858 in the Persian province of Fars. He travelled widely, spending time in Khorasan, Transoxiana, India and Baghdad, and he made the pilgrimage to Mecca three times. A controversial figure even in his own time, he fell foul of the religious authorities, who accused him of blasphemy. His execution in 922 has been widely written about, notably by Attar in his *Tadhkirat al-auliya* (Memorial of the Saints). Like Bistami, Hallāj is celebrated for his ecstatic utterances, the most frequently quoted of which is *'ana 'l-Haqq'* ('I am the Truth', or 'I am God'). As with Bistami, his ecstatic utterances could be interpreted as blasphemy. For some, including Rumi, when Hallāj said 'I am God', there was no 'Hallāj'. He was non-existent.

> On Mansur's lips, 'I am God' was the light of truth.
> 'I am the Lord', on the lips of Pharaoh was a lie.
>
> (M II: 305)

> A midwife might say that the woman has no pain; but pain
> paves the way for the birth of the child.
> The one who is without pain is a thief, because to be
> without pain is to say 'I am God'.
> To say that 'I' at the wrong moment is a curse on the one
> who says it; to say that 'I' in the right moment is a
> blessing from God.
> The 'I' of Mansur became a blessing; the 'I' of Pharaoh
> became a curse.
>
> (M II: 2520–3)

Chapter Five

Rumi's Cast of Characters

The mention of Moses' name is sufficient to shackle our thoughts, for we tend to assume that what we are reading is a retelling of events that happened in the past.

(M III: 1251)

Rumi's writings are peopled with references to figures from the Qur'an and traditional Persian and Arabic folklore, as well as to eminent Sufis from the past: Abraham, Moses, Jesus, Muhammad, Layla and Majnun, Mahmud and Ayaz, Ibrahim ibn Adham, Mansur al-Hallāj, Bayazid Bistami, and many more. In Book III of the *Mathnawi*, Rumi gives the following warning to his readers about his reference to these figures:

The mention of Moses' name is sufficient to shackle our thoughts, for we tend to assume that what we are reading is a retelling of events that happened in the past. The name 'Moses' acts as a mask, concealing from us the 'Light of Moses' which should be our real concern. In fact, the names 'Moses' and 'Pharaoh' refer to aspects of our own being, so when we read of the enmity between them we should look for these two adversaries within ourselves. The Light of Moses has been passed down from generation to generation, and is with us until the Resurrection. Yet the Light itself remains the same; it is the lamp that emits the Light which is different. This earthenware lamp and its wick are different, but the light it emits is no different for it comes from the world beyond this world. If we focus our attention on the glass of the lamp, we will go astray,

> because it is through focusing our attention on the glass
> [the outer form] that we give birth to duality. If we keep
> our attention focused on the Light, we will liberate
> ourselves from the duality and plurality of this seemingly
> finite world. It is this focus of attention that distinguishes
> the true believer from the Zoroastrians and Jews.

> (M III: 1251–8)

Rumi's warning about names shackling our thoughts also applies to his
closing reference to Zoroastrians and Jews. Outwardly, he might
appear to be referring to those people who belong to the two religions;
inwardly he is referring to certain characteristics to be found within
ourselves. In this instance, for example, 'Zoroastrians' and 'Jews' may
be understood metaphorically, as a broader reference to those of us
who adhere to a particular set of strict religious beliefs, or to that aspect
of the individual self that does so. As with the name 'Moses', however,
such adherence can mask the Light. The 'true believer', on the other
hand, is the person (or aspect of the self) that penetrates the outer
form of religious belief and, having passed beyond it, focuses attention
on the Light behind the glass. The Light to which Rumi refers is the
subject of the often-quoted 'Light Verse', from Surah 24 of the Qur'an,
a surah which is itself entitled The Light (*Al-Nur*).

> God is the Light of the heavens and the earth. His Light may
> be compared to a niche in which is a lamp. The lamp is
> enclosed in glass: the glass shines, as it were, like a brilliant
> star, lit from a blessed tree, an olive, neither of the East nor of
> the West, whose oil almost shines forth of itself, though
> untouched by fire. Light upon Light! God guides to His Light
> whom He wills. And God speaks to humankind in allegories, for
> God is Knower of all things.

> (Q 24:35)

Rumi takes up the Qur'anic analogy of the lamp and the Light in a discourse in *Fihi mafihi*, where he explains why analogies are necessary in the expression of spiritual truths.

> Everything I say is an analogy, not an equivalence. An analogy is one thing, an equivalence another. God drew an analogy when He compared His Light to a lamp, and the existence of the saints to the glass of the lamp. This is by way of analogy. The Light of God cannot be contained by the world of created existence, so how then could It be contained in a glass and a lamp? How could the rays of the Light of Almighty God be contained in the heart? Yet when you seek His Light, you find it there. This does not mean that the heart contains the Light. Rather, you find the Light radiating from the heart, just as when you look in a mirror and see an image of yourself. Your image is not contained in the mirror, but when you look in the mirror you see yourself. Those things that appear unintelligible become intelligible when they are expressed as analogies.

> (F 44: A174/T173)

Rumi's cast of characters can therefore be seen as having an underlying meaning. If we focus our attention on their outward form, we will see them as historical figures, or as aspects of ourselves. If we are able to adjust the focus of our attention beyond the outer form, we will see the underlying meaning intended by Rumi. He explains the process by which we can do this in the *Mathnawi*:

> If you wish to pass beyond mere names and letters, purge yourself of self at one stroke . . . Purify yourself of all attributes of self, so that you may see your own pure untarnished essence, and perceive in your heart the knowledge of the prophets, without book, without teacher, without master.

> (M I: 3458, 3460–1)

In other words, the more we are able to rid ourselves of our ego-centred self, with its beliefs, opinions and prejudices, the closer we will come to the source of knowledge that lies concealed beneath the layers of 'self'. It is in this spirit that this chapter explores a few of the principal figures who appear on the stage of Rumi's writings.

THE MESSENGERS

A Messenger is the founder of a new religion whereas a Prophet renews the spiritual message previously revealed by a Messenger. In Rumi's writings, we encounter the four Messengers who appeared in the Near East and laid the foundations of the Abrahamic tradition: Abraham, Moses, Jesus and Muhammad. There have also been other Messengers, the founders of the non-Semitic religions, who have appeared at other times and in other places. It is perhaps to these that the Qur'an refers when God addresses Muhammad, saying, *Of some Messengers We have told you the story. Of others, We have not.* (Q 4:164)

Abraham (Ibrahim)

The Qur'an tells us that Abraham's people worshipped numerous idols instead of the one true God (Q 6:74). They were thus practitioners of polytheism. As part of his drive to convert them to monotheism, Abraham smashed their idols, an act that angered Nimrod, the ruler of the time, who ordered him to be thrown into a fire. However, God's intervention saved Abraham from harm, *We said, 'O fire, be coolness and safety for Abraham'* (Q 21:52–71, 37:83–98). Whilst Abraham's smashing of the idols may appear outwardly to be a significant event in the foundation of the monotheistic Abrahamic religions, it also has an inner sense. Since, in the Islamic tradition 'polytheism' (*shirk*) means to attribute to any being or thing an existence that is outside or independent of the Divine Unity (*tawhid*), in this sense even a mental image of God has the potential to become an idol. Yet herein lies a paradox, as Rumi explains in Book II of the *Mathnawi*.

When the mirror of your heart becomes clear and
pure, you will behold images from beyond this world of
water and clay.

You will behold both the image and the image-
Maker, both the carpet of spiritual reality and the carpet-
Spreader.

The image of the Beloved is like Abraham –
outwardly an idol, inwardly a breaker of idols.

Thanks be to God that when He appeared, the spirit
[within me] beheld its own image in His image.

(M II: 72–5)

Rumi refers again to the paradoxical simultaneity of idol-breaking and
idol-making in verses from the *Divan*, 'Abraham, who broke idols
every year, was by day and night an idol-maker in Thy image-house' (D
772), and again, 'Every idol you have broken, O Abraham, receives life
from that breaking' (D 2006; A2:249). This paradox is implicit in Rumi's
warning concerning the name 'Moses', quoted at the beginning of this
chapter (*see* page 105). For if we perceive Moses solely as an historical
figure, he becomes an idol, a veil between ourselves and the Almighty.
On the other hand, if we are able to pass beyond the outer form and
perceive the inner reality – that is, the 'Light of Moses' – we will
become, like Abraham in the above verse, a 'breaker of idols'.

Abraham's supreme act of idol-breaking is his total surrender to
the Will of God – his *islam* – which is illustrated by his willingness to
subjugate himself to the Divine Command and sacrifice Ishmael, his
son by Hagar, his slave. Indeed, Abraham's *islam* is held up as an
example for others to follow, and Rumi cites it in the story of chickpeas
being cooked in a pot (*see* page 93). In encouraging the chickpeas
(true believers) to allow themselves to be cooked (transformed), the
cook (their teacher) says to them:

'I am Abraham, you are my son. Lay your head under the
knife, *I saw in a vision that I must sacrifice you.* [Q
37:102]

> Lay your head under my rigour, with an easy heart, so
>   that I may cut your throat, like Ishmael's.
> I will cut off your head, although this head is a head
>   unaffected by cutting and dying.
> Yet God's will is that you should submit yourself: Oh
>   Muslim, you must seek to submit yourself to Him.

(M III: 4174–7)

The site where Abraham had made ready to sacrifice his son is marked by the Kaaba, for which Abraham and Ishmael *raised the foundations* (Q 2:127). According to tradition, Abraham lived there for a while. However, for Rumi the Kaaba has an inner meaning: it is the spiritual heart of a human being. It is in this context that Rumi says in the *Divan*, 'Like Abraham, I never turn away from the Kaaba – I reside in the Kaaba, I am its pillar' (D 1747).

God reminds us of the purpose of the Kaaba (or *House* as it is referred to in the Qur'an), saying, *We made the House a place of assembly for mankind and a place of safety, [saying], Take as your place of prayer the station of Abraham* (Q 2:125). In *Fihi mafihi*, Rumi provides us with an explanation of both the outer and inner (or literal and spiritual) meanings of the *station of Abraham*.

> Abraham's station and place of prayer is a certain location near the Kaaba where the literalists say two inclinations (*rak'as*) of prayer must be performed. This is indeed good. But for the mystics Abraham's station means that you should throw yourself into the fire for God's sake, thereby bringing yourself through effort and endeavour to this station, or close to it. You will then have sacrificed yourself for the sake of God – that is to say, you will no longer have any concern or fear for your lower self. To perform two *rak'as* of prayer at Abraham's station is good, but the prayer should be such that the standing part is performed in this world and the prostration in the other world.

(F 44: A173–4/T172)

The fire to which Rumi refers here is the same fire into which Abraham was thrown on the orders of the tyrannical ruler Nimrod after he had destroyed the idols worshipped by Nimrod's people. But it is also more than this.

> This 'fire' is the fire of carnality, within which lie the root
>   of sin and error.
> External fire may be quenched with water, the fire of
>   carnality draws you towards hell.
> What is the remedy for carnality's fire? The light of
>   religion: it will extinguish the fire of the unbelievers.
> What kills this fire? The Light of God. Make the light of
>   Abraham your master.
> So that your body, which can be likened to wood, may be
>   delivered from the fire of your Nimrod-like self.
>
> (M I: 3697–701)

The 'fire' may be equated with the suffering caused by the tug-of-war between our lower and higher selves. As such, it is a natural stage in our spiritual evolution, a stage through which we are required to pass if we wish to liberate ourselves from the tyranny of our lower self. However, fear of the fire – or, rather, the fear of suffering – prevents us from taking this important step. Using the metaphorical imagery of springtime, Rumi reminds us that what may appear outwardly to be a painful experience is essentially a transformational one, 'For the sake of Abraham His friend He causes the fire to burn, and converts Nimrod's furnace into blossoms and eglantine' (D 528: A1:63).

This adversarial relationship between Abraham (our light-bearing aspect) and Nimrod (our ego-centred self) is echoed in Rumi's references to the three other Messengers, Moses, Jesus and Muhammad. In Moses' case, it is Pharaoh, the ruler of Egypt; for Jesus, it is his donkey or ass; for Muhammad, it is Abu Jahl.

Moses (Musa)

Like Abraham before him, Moses, the founding father of Judaism, also
has to face the fire. In Moses' case, however, the fire takes the form of
an encounter with a burning bush, as related in the Book of Exodus
(3:1ff) and the Qur'an (20:9ff; 27:7–14; 28:29–35). In his writings, Rumi
returns repeatedly to the rich imagery of the Qur'anic accounts of
the incident, of which the following passage from Surah 20, one of the
earliest to be revealed at Mecca, is an example. Moses, who is travelling
with his people, has seen a fire in the distance. Commanding his
kinfolk to wait for him, he tells them that he will go to the fire in the
hope of finding guidance there, or, failing this, that he will bring back
some of the fire so that they may warm themselves. The passage opens
with Moses approaching the bush and God calling him by his name:

> 'O Moses! Behold, I am your Lord. So take off thy shoes, for
> thou art in the sacred valley of Tuwa. Know that I have chosen
> thee. Therefore listen to what shall be revealed. I am Allah.
> There is no god but Me. Serve Me alone, and establish prayers
> in remembrance of Me. Behold, the Hour is coming, but I
> choose to keep it hidden, so that every soul may be rewarded
> according to its endeavour. Therefore let not thy thoughts be
> turned aside by those who disbelieve and indulge their desires,
> lest thou perish. And what is that in thy right hand, O Moses?'
> He said, 'It is my staff, on which I lean, and with which I beat
> down branches for my flock, and for which I find other uses.'
> He [Allah] said, 'Cast it down, O Moses!' So he cast it down,
> and behold, it was a gliding serpent. He [Allah] said, 'Take hold
> of it, and fear not. We shall return it to its former state. Now
> put thy hand under thy armpit: it will come forth white [and
> shining], and unharmed. This shall be another sign.'

(Q 20:11–22)

Rumi explains the inner meaning of this conversation between God and
Moses in the following extract from a poem from the *Divan* which
contains a number of familiar themes: the Light, the relinquishing of
duality, the abandonment of our supports (our beliefs and concepts),

and the idea of suffering as a gateway to freedom. It is also an appropriate point at which to remind ourselves of Rumi's warning about not allowing our thoughts to be shackled by the name 'Moses'. In the *Mathnawi*, he reiterates the warning in more explicit terms with reference to Moses' staff, 'For us, the name of everything expresses its outer appearance; for the Creator, the name of everything expresses its inner reality. In Moses' eyes the name of his rod was "staff"; in the Creator's eyes its name was "serpent".' (M I: 1239–40) This reversal of perception is a key element in the following verses.

> When Moses saw the Light from the bush, he said, 'My
>   search is over, for I have been granted this gift.'
> God said, 'O Moses, cease your wandering! *Throw down*
>   *thy staff!*' [Q 28:31]
> Moses straightway cast from his heart kinfolk, friends, and
>   companions.
> This is the meaning of *Put off thy two shoes!* [Q 20:12]
>   'Sever thy love from the two worlds!'
> The house of the heart has room for none but God . . .
> God said, '*O Moses, what is that in thy hand?*' Moses said,
>   '*That is my staff* for the road' [Q 20:17–18].
> He said, '*Cast it down* [Q 20:19] and see the wonders of
>   heaven!'
> He threw it down, and it became a gliding serpent [Q
>   20:20]; when he saw the serpent, he fled.
> God said, '*Take hold of it and I will return it to its former*
>   *state*' [Q 20:21]:
> 'I will make your enemy your helper, and your adversary
>   your support . . .
> When We inflict pain on your hands and feet, they
>   become serpents in your eyes.
> O hand, grasp nothing but Us! O foot, seek nothing but
>   the Goal!
> Do not flee from the suffering We inflict, for where there
>   is suffering there is also a way to relief.'

(D 123, after Chittick, *The Sufi Path of Love*, p. 297)

The idea that our enemy may be our helper was encountered earlier, when Abraham was cast into the furnace by Nimrod, his adversary. What appeared outwardly to be a horrendous experience was inwardly the moment of Abraham's transformation. In another poem from the *Divan*, Rumi describes Moses' encounter with the burning bush in a similar vein: the remedy for our human predicament lies in confronting the fire of suffering head on, not in turning away from it.

> When Moses advanced towards the burning bush,
> the bush said, 'I am the water of Kauthar, *Take off thy*
> *shoes* [Q 20:12], and come.
> Fear not my fire, for I am sweet water. Good
> fortune and the seat of honour are yours.
> You are a lustrous pearl, a ruby of the mine, the
> soul of place and placelessness; you are without equal in
> this age; how can other beings compare with you?'
>
> (D 45: A1:6)

The water (or waters) of Kauthar, which Rumi mentions often in his writings, is a reference to a fountain in Paradise which is the subject of an eponymous surah in the Qur'an, Surah 108, *Al-Kauthar* or Abundance. As before, the implication here is that the Divine Command '*take off thy shoes*' is a call to Moses to cast off the dualism of the two worlds. In doing so, he will discover his true nature and the infinite abundance that lies within him. But as Rumi reminds us in other poems from the *Divan*, when he is talking about Moses, he is referring to our own inner reality.

> Who is there who . . .
> . . . like Moses looking for fire,
> comes across a bush,
> goes to gather fire from it,
> and discovers myriad dawns and sunrises.
>
> (D 598: A1:74)

Come, O soul! You are Moses,
your bodily form is your staff:
grasp hold of me, I am a staff;
thrown me down, I am a serpent.

(D 1414: A1:172)

Another episode from the Qur'anic accounts of the life of Moses to
which Rumi refers frequently is the epiphany on Mount Sinai. The
Qur'an relates that when Moses came to the place appointed by God,
he asked Him to reveal Himself so that he could see Him face to face.
God replied,

'Thou shalt not see Me, but look upon the mountain; if it
remains firm in its place, then thou shalt see Me.' And when
God revealed Himself to the mountain, He crushed it to dust.
Moses fell down senseless, and when he recovered his senses,
he said, 'Glory be to Thee! To Thee I turn in repentance, and I
am the first of believers.'

(Q 7:144–5)

As Rumi explains,

Hidden things are revealed by means of their opposite;
since God has no opposite, He remains hidden . . . The
Light of God has no opposite within existence by means of
which, through its opposite, it might be made manifest.
Therefore our eyes cannot see Him, but He sees all eyes [Q
6: 104]. Understand this from Moses at Mount Sinai.'

(M 1: 1131, 1134–5)

In a poem from the *Divan*, Rumi provides us with a powerful analogy
that we can apply to our own wandering along life's path. For the Sufi,
who is the 'child of the present moment', the goal of our journey does
not lie at some distant point in future time. It is forever present.

Know that the world is like Mount Sinai,
and we, like Moses, are seekers;
every moment there is a revelation
that splits the mountain apart.

(D 14: A1:2)

MOSES AND PHARAOH

The manner in which 'hidden things are revealed by means of their
opposites' is played out in Rumi's portrayal of the interaction between
Moses (as Messenger and archetype of the enlightened soul) and
Pharaoh (as worldly ruler and archetype of the ego-centred soul). The
roles of the two adversaries are succinctly stated in the Qur'an, where
we are told that God sent Moses to Pharaoh to ask him if he wished to
reform and be guided to his Lord. As proof of God's almighty power,
Moses showed him *a great sign*, but Pharaoh rejected it, summoned
his people together, and addressed them, proclaiming, *'I am your
Lord, the Highest'* (Q 79:24). Rumi comments on the inner significance
of Pharaoh's proclamation:

God's generosity has endowed us with a Pharaohship,
but not one that perishes like Pharaoh and his kingdom.
You who have been misled by Egypt and the Nile,
raise your eyes and see the glorious living kingdom.
If you wish to quit this soiled and tattered garment,
drown the bodily Nile in the Nile of the Spirit.

Listen, O Pharaoh, let go of Egypt!
Within the Egypt of the Spirit lie a hundred Egypts.
You say to the people, 'I am Lord', whilst ignorant
of the essential nature of 'I' and 'Lord'.
How could a Lord be affected by that which he overlords?
How could one who knows 'I' be bound by body and soul?
We are the real 'I', having been freed from the false 'I',
from the 'I' that is full of suffering and strife.

(M V: 4124–30)

Elsewhere in the *Mathnawi*, Rumi tells us that although Moses and Pharaoh are both subject to the Divine Will, they are like antidote and poison, darkness and light (M I, between 2446 and 2447). He then employs the metaphor of the game of polo, in which the Divine decree *'Be, and it is'* is likened to a polo mallet that has propelled us, like a ball struck by the mallet, into the phenomenal world of time and space. Prior to this, we were at liberty to roll freely in space and spacelessness. But since colourlessness (the Divine Unity) became imprisoned in the colours of the phenomenal world, 'a Moses came into conflict with a Moses' (M I: 2466-7). The paradox of this last statement is explained succinctly by Franklin D. Lewis, 'smacked forward into the visible spectrum of creation, we are tinged with attributes that bring us into conflict and opposition' (Lewis, *Rumi*, p. 414). To remind us that things are never quite as they appear to be, Rumi employs the metaphor of wearing our shoes on the wrong feet. In reality, he says, 'the rebelliousness of Pharaoh was caused by Moses' (M I: 2481); or, as Professor Nicholson explains, Pharaoh's rebelliousness 'was the effect of the inward repudiation of Pharaoh by Moses, who was his opposite' (Nicholson, *Mathnawi*, vol. II, p. 135). However, the opposition between the Moses and Pharaoh within us ends when we shed the all-too-human attributes we have taken on and regain our original 'colourless' state. Then, as Rumi says, 'Moses and Pharaoh are at peace with each other' (M I: 2469).

> The Moses-soul pulls out
> the moustache of the Pharaoh-body,
> so that the body becomes all soul,
> alive to the tip of every hair.

(D 1131: A1:143)

Jesus (Isa)

The high regard in which Jesus is held by Muslims and Sufis alike has its foundations in the Qur'an, where he is referred to as *the Messiah . . . a Messenger of God, and His Word which He bestowed on Mary, and a Spirit from Him* (Q 4:171).

The story of the birth of Jesus as told in the Qur'an differs in certain aspects from the traditional sequence of events narrated in the New Testament gospels. An example of these differences is to be found in the following passage from Surah 19, which tells of the birth of Jesus taking place beneath a palm tree. (A similar episode involving a palm tree appears in the *Gospel of Pseudo-Matthew*, dating from the eighth or ninth centuries, although there it is set after the birth of Jesus, during his family's journey into Egypt.) The passage opens with Mary's response when Gabriel, the heavenly messenger, appeared before her:

> We sent unto her Our spirit in the form of a perfect man. And when she saw him, she said, 'I seek refuge from you in the Merciful One. If you fear the Lord, go on your way.'
>
> He said, 'I am only a messenger from your Lord, that I may bestow on you a faultless son.'
>
> She said, 'How shall I have a son since no man has touched me, neither am I unchaste?'
>
> He said, 'Such is the will of your Lord, who says, "It is easy for Me. He shall be a sign for humankind and a Mercy from Us. It is so decreed."'
>
> And she conceived him, and withdrew to a far off place. And the pangs of childbirth drove her to the trunk of a palm tree. She cried out, 'Oh, would that I had died before this! Would that I had passed into oblivion, forgotten!'
>
> Then a voice called out from beneath her, saying, 'Do not grieve! Your Lord has placed a rivulet beneath you. And shake the trunk of the palm tree, it will drop fresh ripe dates into your lap. So eat and drink, and rejoice.'

(Q 19:17–26)

The story of Gabriel's visit to Mary is retold by Rumi in a passage in the *Mathnawi*, but he begins by applying Mary's words to Gabriel in a very different context. Addressing his audience directly, he writes, 'Before everything you own slips away, be like Mary, say to the material world, "I seek refuge from you with the Merciful One"' (M III: 3700). Or, as

Coleman Barks writes in his rendition of the same verse, 'say what Mary said . . . "I'll hide inside God"' (Barks, *One-Handed Basket Weaving*, p. 31). In effect, Rumi is reminding us that we have a choice between the temporary security offered by our material possessions and the permanent security offered by God, two of whose Divine Names are *al-Muhaymin* and *al-Hafiz* (the Protector, and the Guardian).

Later on in the same passage, Rumi repeats Mary's words in their original context. At the same time he reiterates the idea that the only source of protection from the transient nature of our this-worldly existence is to be found in God:

> Mary became self-less, and in this selfless state she said, "I
> will leap into God's protection,"
> because that pure-bosomed one was accustomed to
> seeking refuge in the Unseen.
> Since she considered this world transient, she made the
> Presence her fortress,
> so that in the hour of death she would have a bastion that
> could withstand any attack.

> (M III: 3707–10)

We saw earlier how Rumi used the examples of Abraham and Moses to show that suffering is an essential part of the transformational process. In Discourse Five of *Fihi mafihi*, he employs the imagery of the birth under the palm tree to make the same point. Rumi brings his discourse to a close with some lines by the Sufi poet Khaqani (1121–99).

> Human beings have a sure guide in everything they
> undertake. Until they experience an ache – a yearning for a
> thing – within themselves, they will never strive to attain it.
> Without pain your goal will remain unattainable, whether it
> be in this world or the next, whether you aim to be a
> merchant or a monarch, a scholar, or an astronomer. It was
> not until Mary experienced the pains of labour that she

went to the tree: *and the pangs of childbirth drove her to the trunk of a palm tree* [Q 19:23]. Pain brought her to the tree, and the barren tree bore fruit. Our body is like Mary. We each have a Jesus within us, but until we feel the birth pains within us our Jesus will not be born. If there are no birth pains, our Jesus will return to his origin by the same hidden path by which he came, and we will remain deprived of him.

The soul within you is neglected;
the body without is well provided.
The demon stuffs itself until it vomits;
Jamshid has not even bread to eat.
Heal your soul while your Jesus is on earth;
for when Jesus returns to heaven
all hope of healing will have gone.

(F 5: A33/T22–3)

(The Jamshid referred to by Khaqani was a mythical Persian king, the Iranian equivalent of Solomon. His pairing here with the demon is explained by Wheeler Thackston: 'Jamshid is contrasted with the *dev* or demon, because, like Solomon, he commanded the djinn as well as men.' Thackston, *Signs of the Unseen*, p. 254)

Conceived by the Spirit or Breath of God, Jesus was granted the gift of giving life and healing the sick through his breath. He announces this gift while still in his cradle, saying, '*Behold, I bring you a sign from your Lord. I will make for you out of clay the likeness of a bird. I shall breathe into it and it shall become, by God's leave, a living bird. By God's leave, I shall heal the blind, and the leper, and raise the dead* (Q 3:49). Taking up this theme in an ode from the *Divan*, Rumi reminds us of the divine origin of the soul by presenting us with an image of Jesus as the Spirit or Breath of God within the soul, and the bird of clay as a metaphor for the human body.

Come, soul! . . .
You are Jesus and I am your bird;
you made a bird out of clay;
when you breathe into me,
I take wing for the highest.

(D 1414: AI:172)

The quotation from the Qur'an makes it abundantly clear that Jesus'
life-giving breath emanates from God. So does Rumi:

Like Jesus, Thy image goes into the heart to bestow a
    new spirit . . .

(D 1847; Chittick, *The Sufi Path of Love*, p. 264)

JESUS AND HIS ASS
Like other figures in Rumi's cast of characters, the role played by Jesus
may vary from one context to another. As Rumi constantly reminds us,
we get to know a thing by its opposite. Where the figure of Jesus is
concerned, we get to know him – or, rather, what he symbolizes – by
getting to know his ass. And by getting to know these two we also get
to know ourselves, for Jesus personifies our higher self (the spirit
within us) while his ass represents our lower self (the carnal self and/or
the ego).

The extreme contrast between these two seems to have
delighted Rumi, for he exploits it to the full, sometimes in lengthy
passages, at other times in brief but pithy asides. An example of the
latter is to be found in Book IV of the *Mathnawi*, where, in advising us
to learn to discriminate between two types of intoxication – the one
spiritually induced, the other induced by the world of phenomena –
Rumi writes, 'Listen, O heart, do not be deceived by every kind of
intoxication: Jesus gets drunk on God, his ass gets drunk on barley' (M
IV: 2691). Sometimes Rumi is even more blunt: 'How could Jesus eat
from the same trough as his ass?' (D 1196: Chittick, *The Sufi Path of
Love*, p. 340).

If the breath of Jesus can bring new life to the ailing soul of the lover, so can his lips – lips which, like those of the Beloved, taste as sweet as sugar. Such imagery provides Rumi with the basis for a powerful metaphor to drive home the contrast between the spiritual and material worlds, between the life of the soul and the life of the body: 'Those who kiss the ass's arse will not be blessed with the sweet kisses of Jesus.' (D 96: after Schimmel, *Rumi's World*, p. 122)

In order to make a particular point, Rumi does not hesitate to employ language that some may find offensive. Yet in its own way his juxtaposition of the words 'Jesus' and 'arse' gives us a yardstick to measure the degree to which our own eyes are focused on either the material or the spiritual world. Which has the greater significance for us, the words or what they transmit? Rumi himself provides the answer to this question: 'When you discover the kernel and have learned to disregard the shell, when you have entered the realm of Jesus, you will no longer say, "Where is my ass?"' (D 1380: A1:169)

And, as Rumi explains in the *Mathnawi*, those who nurture the Jesus within them have a lean ass and the rest of us have a fat one.

> By abandoning Jesus you have nurtured his ass. So, like the
>   ass, you remain on the other side of the curtain.
> Knowledge and gnosis are the property of Jesus, not of
>   the ass. Oh, you asinine fool!
> You hear the ass moaning, and you take pity on it; that's
>   how the ass gets you to behave like an ass.
> Have pity on Jesus, not on the ass! Don't let your animal
>   nature rule your intellect . . .
> For donkey's years you've been the slave of the ass. But
>   that's long enough, for the ass's slave trails along
>   behind the ass.
> When the Prophet said, 'Put the women behind you!', he
>   meant your ego-centred self. For it must be put last,
>   and your intellect first.
> Your base intellect has taken on the characteristics of an
>   ass. Its only thought is, 'How shall I find fodder?'
> Jesus' ass took on the characteristics of the spirit. It made

its home where intelligence dwells.
Because the spiritual intellect was in command, the ass
    was weak. A strong rider has a lean ass!
Yet because your intellect is weak . . . your worn-out ass
    has become a dragon.

(M II: 1850–3, 1855–60)

As we shall see in the next chapter, Rumi's use of the ass to symbolize the material world or the baser instincts within us is not always linked with the figure of Jesus.

JESUS AND THE SPREAD TABLE
The opening verses of Surah 5 of the Qur'an, titled 'The Table', set out which foods are lawful and which are unlawful for Muslims to eat. The subject of food also features in the closing verses where we are told how Jesus' disciples asked him if God could *send down a table spread with food from heaven* [Q 5:112] so that they might *eat of it and satisfy their hearts* [Q 5:113]. Jesus asked God, saying, *O Lord, send down to us a table spread with food from heaven, that it may be a feast for us, for the first of us and the last of us, and a sign from Thee. Give us sustenance, for Thou art the Best of Sustainers* [Q 5:114]. And God sent down the Table.

In brief, the Surah leads us from the material to the spiritual world. It begins with the laws relating to the material food we ingest and ends by informing us that the true source of our sustenance lies on the spiritual plane. Rumi's references to the Spread Table, or sometimes simply to the Table, generally serve to remind us of the choice that constantly faces us: do we rely on the phenomenal world for our food – whether this be physical, mental or spiritual – or do we fast from it and in so doing turn to the Divine Generosity?

The act of renouncing our reliance on the phenomenal world is depicted by Rumi as an act of cleansing, a necessary prerequisite if we are to feed from the Table. It is also the moment at which we are united with the Jesus within us. He greets us, saying 'Welcome! Wash your hands and mouth, for now the Table is spread' (D 446: A1:52).

In another ode from the *Divan*, the ass puts in a further appearance:

> When Jesus got rid of his ass, his prayers were accepted;
> wash your hands, for the Table has come down from
>   heaven.

> (D 892: A1:115)

So much for renouncing this world and the ego. But what does the other world have to offer? Rumi's answer is succinct:

> When you fast, await the arrival of the Table of
>   Generosity,
> for the Table of Generosity is better than stewed cabbage'

> (D 1739: A2:217)

THE PROPHET MUHAMMAD

The Prophet Muhammad occupies a central place in the life of all Muslims, for he taught them the religion of *islam*, leaving clear guidelines for them to follow in the *Sunnah* (the Traditions and teachings of the Prophet). He is also the model of the perfected human being on which true Muslims base the way in which they conduct their lives. As such, the presence of the Prophet permeates Rumi's writings, either directly or by allusion. The name 'Muhammad' translates as 'the most praised one', but Rumi also refers to him by a number of the Prophet's Divine Names, notably 'Ahmad' ('the most praiseworthy of those who praise Allah') and 'Mustafa' ('the divinely elected') (Bayrak, *The Most Beautiful Names*, pp. 143, 157).

The life of the Prophet was discussed earlier (*see* pages 53–67) and the influence of his presence and teaching will be found throughout Rumi's writings presented in this book. Consequently, this section is brief and comprises two passages from *Fihi mafihi* to illustrate the centrality of the Prophet in Rumi's life and teachings. The third passage is from the *Mathnawi*, and relates an incident which, according to Rumi, was the origin of the Tradition that the unbeliever takes his food in seven bowls, while the true believer takes his food in one bowl. In this last passage, Rumi refers to the Prophet by his name of Mustafa.

> . . . if a branch is laden with fruit, it pulls the branch down, whereas a branch that bears no fruit holds its head up high, like a poplar tree. When a branch is excessively laden with fruit, props are put under it so that it is not completely weighed down.
>
> The Prophet was extremely humble, because all the fruits of this world and the next were gathered upon him. He was thus the most humble of men. 'No one was able to precede the Messenger of God in making a greeting.' That is, no one was able to offer greetings before the Prophet because the Prophet, being extremely humble, would always greet the other first. Even supposing he did not greet the other first, the Prophet was still the humble one and the first to offer greetings, because others had learned the manner of greeting from him. Whether in ancient times or latterly, everything that human beings possess is a reflection of him, and his shadow. A man's shadow may enter a house ahead of him, but in reality the man is ahead of his shadow even though it appears to the eye as though his shadow precedes him. For even though the shadow may precede the man, it is derived from him . . .
>
> It is acknowledged that Muhammad was the origin, for God said, 'But for thee, I would not have created the heavens.' Every thing that exists – nobility, humility, authority and elevated station – all are his gift, and his shadow, for they were all manifested through him.
>
> (F 25: A116, 117/T109–10)

A person said, 'I have a certain state in which there is no room for either Muhammad or the cherubim.'

It is amazing that a servant of God should have a state in which there is no room for Muhammad! Muhammad does not have a state in which there is no room for a wretched creature like you! . . . After all, this spiritual state you have attained is entirely due to him [Muhammad] and his influence. All gifts are first showered upon him, then they are distributed through him to others. That is the way it is. God said, 'O Prophet, peace be upon you, and God's mercy. We have showered upon you all gifts.' Muhammad added, 'And upon God's righteous servants!'

The way to God is extremely fearful, blocked and full of snow. Muhammad was the first to risk his life, driving his horse forward to open the road. Whoever travels this road, does so by his guidance and protection. For he was the first to discover the way, and he left signposts everywhere, 'Do not go in this direction,' and 'Do not go in that direction,' and 'If you go in that direction, you will perish like the people of 'Ad and Thamud [two peoples, mentioned in the Qur'an, whose sinfulness incurred God's wrath and who were destroyed]', and 'If you go in this direction, you will be saved, like the believers.' . . .

Know that Muhammad is the guide. Until a person has first reached Muhammad, he cannot reach Us.'

(F 63: A232/T235, 236)

One evening, a group of infidels came to the Prophet's mosque asking for hospitality. The Prophet instructed his Companions to take the infidels into their homes as honoured guests. Among the unbelievers was a stout man with a huge body. Since none of the Companions chose to take him into their home, he remained behind in the mosque, like the dregs left in the bottom of a cup. The Prophet therefore took him into his own home, where the large man devoured all the food put before him and drank all the milk from the Prophet's seven milking goats. This angered some members of the Prophet's household who had to go without goat's milk. Having consumed enough food for eighteen people, the large guest went to bed. The maid, who was still resentful about the goat's milk, fastened the door of his room from the outside with a chain. During the night, the infidel developed a stomach-ache and felt an urgent need to relieve himself. He tried to open the door but, finding it shut, went back to bed. In his sleep he dreamt he was in a desolate place, and so he relieved himself only to awaken and find that he had soiled his clothes. Beside himself with shame, he bemoaned his disgrace, saying, 'My sleep is worse than my waking state: with the one I eat but with the other I excrete!' He waited for the night to end, hoping that when the door was opened he would be able to get away without anyone seeing him in such a state.

Mustafa came at dawn and opened the door to this lost soul. He became hidden so that the man would not be shamed and could walk forth boldly, without having to face the door-opener. Mustafa either hid himself behind something, or God's mercy concealed him from the infidel. He saw what had befallen the man during the night, but the Hand of God restrained him from letting the man out before he had disgraced himself. Divine wisdom decreed that the man should thus see himself in this state. Later, a meddling busybody brought the soiled bedding to the Prophet, saying, 'Look at what your guest has done!' Mustafa smiled, and said, 'Bring a bowl, that I may wash these things clean myself.'

Noticing that he had lost an amulet, the wretched infidel returned to Mustafa's house and found him washing the soiled bedding. All thought of the amulet vanished from his mind. Tearing his clothes, he prostrated himself before Mustafa, saying, 'You, who are the Whole, surrender to His Will; I am but an insignificant and misguided part.' The man began to tremble violently, and Mustafa took him in his arms. When he had calmed him down, he opened the man's inner eye and gave him spiritual knowledge . . .

When the body empties itself of dung, God fills it with musk and precious pearls.

(abridged from M V: 65–148)

FIGURES FROM THE QUR'AN

Joseph (Yusuf), son of Jacob

Many will already be familiar with events from the biblical account of
the life of Joseph: his being cast into a well by his brothers, his
attempted seduction by Potiphar's wife, his imprisonment, his
interpretation of Pharaoh's dreams, and his rise to a position of
prominence in Egypt. The events related in the Qur'an are similar to
these, but one particular episode caught the imagination of the Persian
poets: the story of Joseph and Zulaykha (the name given in Islamic
legend to the biblical 'Potiphar's wife'), which has become one of the
great love stories of the Islamic world. Like other love stories favoured
by the Sufis, the story of Joseph and Zulaykha is an allegory of the lover
and the Beloved in which Joseph is the embodiment of Divine beauty.
Zulaykha's passionate love for Joseph became a subject for gossip
among the women of Egypt, and so to stem the gossip Zulaykha
arranged for him to appear at a banquet as the women were cutting
their fruit. His beauty was such that the women were distracted and
cut their hands (see Qur'an 12:30–1). It is to this that Rumi alludes in
a poem from the *Divan*.

> O Beautiful One! Repair this ruin with a glance of your
> eye.
> In the tomb of the body, heart and soul are martyrs to
> your love.
> Come, pass by this martyrs' tomb!
> Like a Joseph, you are come, and all Egypt cut its hands.
> Reveal your charms, and take my heart and soul.

> (D 1986: A2/246)

This reference to the 'tomb of the body' is a theme Rumi often
associates with Joseph's imprisonment by Pharaoh, as here in the
Mathnawi.

The house of the heart that is unlit by the rays of the
Divine Sun is dark and bleak, deprived of spiritual love. A
tomb is better than such a heart. Come! Arise from the
tomb of your heart! Are you not suffocating in this
cramped tomb? You are the Joseph of the age and
heaven's sun. Arise from this pit and prison and show
your face!

(M II: 3129–34)

A similar symbolism is associated with the well into which Joseph was
thrown by his brothers (see page 61). A contrasting imagery is
provided by Rumi's references to the robe Joseph gave to his brothers
when they visited him in Egypt. He told them to take it home with
them and cast it over the head of Jacob, his blind father, who would
thus regain his sight. When the caravan left Egypt, Jacob declared, 'I
scent the presence of Joseph' (Q 12:94), and on the brothers' return he
threw Joseph's robe over his head and was indeed able to see again (Q
12:96). In the same way that Jacob sensed Joseph's presence from the
scent of his robe, Rumi encourages us to 'scent' the Presence of God
so that our spiritual eyes might be opened.

I told the secret of union with the Beloved to none
but the breeze. The breeze said in its innermost heart –
'Like this.'
    In spite of those who say, 'How do we attain union
with God?' keep your eyes fastened on the light – 'Like
this.'
    I said, 'How does the scent of Joseph travel from
town to town?' The scent of God breathed from the world
of He – 'Like this.'
    I said, 'How does the scent of Joseph restore
sight?' Your breeze wafted over my eyes – 'Like this.'

(D 1826: A2/226)

Make the scent of Joseph's robe your rope.
Hold fast to it, for his scent gives sight to the eyes.

(M IV: 3221)

Solomon

Solomon is renowned for his wisdom and the miraculous powers he
had over human beings, the jinn and the animals. In the Qur'an, he
declares, *'O people! We have been taught the language of the birds'* (Q
27:16). Sufis interpret the language of the birds as meaning 'the
language of the divine mysteries or of the birds of the spirit which fly
in God's Presence' (Chittick, *The Sufi Path of Love*, p. 353). (For more
on birds as symbols of the soul, *see* page 150.)

When Solomon's tent was pitched, the birds came to pay
    their respects.
They found him speaking the same language as
    themselves, and one by one they sped into his
    presence.
The birds ceased their twittering and became more
    articulate in Solomon's presence.
Speaking the same language is brotherhood and affinity:
    when we can't converse, we're like a prisoner in
    chains.

(M I: 1202–5)

Until the spiritual Solomon, skilled in tongues, intervenes,
    duality will not pass away.
O you argumentative birds! Be like the falcon,
    listen to the falcon drum of the King . . .
We are like blind birds, clumsy and inept,
    for we have not recognized Solomon.

(M II: 3742–3, 3746)

Khidr

Khidr, the immortal 'green man' – one of the most enigmatic figures of Islamic tradition – is said to have drunk from the Water of Life. He appears in the Qur'an, although not referred to by name, where we are told that God *had taught him knowledge from Our Presence* (Q 18:66). Moses, in search of knowledge of God, asks Khidr to be his guide, saying, *May I follow thee, so that thou mayst teach me what thou hast been taught?* (Q 18:67). Khidr accepts. Aware of Moses' lack of understanding of the workings of the Divine Unity, Khidr warns him not to question anything that happens. He must be patient, for Khidr will explain everything to him in due course. The two men set off, and the ensuing events are so bizarre that Moses is unable to restrain himself from questioning Khidr's actions, pronouncing them to be evil or, at best, unreasonable. Indeed, Khidr's actions would inspire a similar response in most of us, for when the two are travelling by boat, Khidr makes a hole in it, causing it to sink; they meet a certain young man, and Khidr kills him; they ask some townspeople for food and lodging, and when they refuse Khidr repairs their wall without asking for payment. When, in spite of having been instructed not to do so, Moses questions Khidr for the third time, the latter tells him that the time has come for them to go their separate ways. However, before they part Khidr explains to Moses the reason for his actions (Q 18:79–83).

The story of Khidr and Moses serves as a model for the relationship between the Sufi shaykh (*pir* or *murshid*) and his disciple (*murid* or *dervish*). Rumi explains this relationship in a passage from Book I of the *Mathnawi*, in which the Prophet Muhammad advises 'Ali (the Prophet's cousin and son-in-law) against relying on his own strength and courage to fight the Greater Holy War. Rather, he should seek out a person of knowledge and place himself under his protective guidance. Of all the devotional acts performed by those who travel the Path, Muhammad tells him, the greatest is to place oneself under the protection of one who serves none but God.

When you have been accepted by the Pir,
obey, and surrender yourself to him;
be like Moses,
submit to the guidance of Khidr.
Whatever your Khidr may do,
be patient. Don't make him say,
'Go, *this is our parting.*'
If he scuttles a boat, say nothing;
if he kills a child, don't tear your hair out.
The hand of the Pir is the Hand of God,
for He said, *the Hand of God is over their hands* [Q 48:10].
This 'Hand of God' slays his *murid*,
who is then reborn as eternal spirit.

(M I: 2969–73)

SEMI-MYTHICAL FIGURES

Layla and Majnun

Dating from pre-Islamic times, the story of Layla and Majnun was transformed through the verses of Arab and Persian poets and has come to epitomize the quest of the lover for the Beloved. The story tells how two beautiful children – Layla (meaning 'night') and Qays (whose name is changed later to Majnun) – were born into different tribes. They fell deeply in love, but when news of their love reached the ears of Layla's father, he confined his daughter to the family tent and banned Qays from entering the tribal encampment. The distraught Qays roamed the neighbourhood, hoping to catch a glimpse of his beloved Layla who had become his only thought. It was now that Qays underwent a change of name: his obsession for Layla was such that people began to call him *Majnun*, 'madman'. In their enforced separation, the two lovers communicated with each other on the wind: throwing love poems in the air hoping they would be carried, like birds on the wing, to their beloved, or they breathed in the wind deeply hoping to catch their beloved's scent.

In his desperation to see Layla, one day Majnun draped himself with a sheep's skin and bribed the shepherd to drive his flock past Layla's tent. Majnun lifted up the tent flap, saw the hem of his beloved's skirt, and fainted. After this, Layla's father placed a guard around the tent, and the lovesick Majnun withdrew into the mountains. Meanwhile, Layla's father arranged for her marriage to another man, but her love for Majnun prevented any intimacy with him. When her husband died some years later, Layla appeared outwardly to be grief-stricken, but inwardly her tears were her way of mourning the years of separation from her real love, Majnun. Many years later, the lovers were finally reunited in death.

Rumi generally employs the story of Layla and Majnun to illustrate how our prolonged separation from the Beloved inspires within us a profound yearning, a desire to be reunited with Him. Since we are not normally aware of the inner reasons for this yearning, our ego is able to commandeer it and turn it into a desire for external, material things, which are the only things the ego can relate to. This state of affairs is encapsulated in the story of Majnun and his camel (see page 150), and in the following passage from a discourse in *Fihi mafihi*.

> Whoever is loved is beautiful, but the reverse is not necessarily true: it does not follow that anyone who is beautiful is loved. Beauty is a part of being loved. As being loved is the root, when an object is loved it follows that it is beautiful. The part cannot be separated from the whole since it derives from the whole.
>
> In Majnun's time there were girls who were much more beautiful than Layla, but they were not loved by Majnun. People used to say to him, 'There are girls more beautiful than Layla. Let us bring them to you.'
>
> 'I do not love Layla for her external appearance,' Majnun would reply. 'Layla is not external form. She is like a drinking vessel held in my hand, a beaker from which I drink wine. I am in love with the wine I drink from the beaker, but you see only the beaker and not the wine. If I had a golden beaker studded with precious gems, and it

were filled with vinegar or something other than wine, of
what use would that beaker be to me? To my eyes a broken
old gourd filled with wine is better than a hundred such
goblets.'

You need love's yearning to see the difference
between the wine and the beaker.

(F 16: A83/T7475; see also M V: 3286–99)

Although Rumi's reference to a certain character may be little more
than a passing allusion, in such instances it is helpful to remind
ourselves of the underlying qualities or state of being with which Rumi
has endowed this character in the wider body of his writings. In the
following verses from the *Divan*, which are about allowing love's
yearning to go unrestrained, Majnun is the 'madman' referred to in
line six; Rumi's reference to the spider in line ten is explained below.

If you are a lover of Love, and seek Love,
take a sharp knife and cut the throat of constraint.
Concern with what others may think of you
hinders your progress along the Path –
I say this impartially, receive it with an open mind.
What caused the madman to perform acts of madness?
That wild one to invent a thousand acts of guile?
He tore his clothes, raced over mountains,
drank poison, and sought annihilation.
If a spider could ensnare so large a prey,
think what prey *My Lord the Most High* [Q 79:24] will take!
If the love of Layla's face was worth this much,
how will it be with *He took His servant by night* [Q 17:1]?

(D 213: A1:26)

The spider is the one that spun a web across the mouth of the cave in
which Muhammad sought refuge on his way from Mecca to Medina
(*see* page 65). The 'large prey' alludes therefore to the Prophet
Muhammad. The words from the Qur'an in the last line are from the

opening of the Qur'anic account of the Night Journey (*mi'raj*) of the Prophet (*see* page 63). (As mentioned above, the name Layla translates as 'night'.)

The relationship between Layla and Majnun, between lover and the Beloved, is encapsulated in the words of Majnun:

> 'I am a lover . . .
> Those who are enlightened
> know that Layla and I
> are one and the same.'

(M V: 2016, 2019)

Mahmud and Ayaz

Another famous love story to which Rumi refers, either directly or by allusion, is that of the relationship between Sultan Mahmud of Ghazna (971–1030) and Ayaz, his devoted Turkish slave. Mahmud himself was the son of a Turkish slave, Sebuktigin, who in 977 became ruler of Ghazna, an area comprising modern Afghanistan and north-eastern Iran. Mahmud, who succeeded his father in 998, was renowned both for his military exploits and as an important patron of art and literature. The relationship between Ayaz and Mahmud, the slave and his master, serves as a model for the relationship between the true believer and God. The true believer's total obedience to the Will of God is illustrated by the story of Ayaz and the king's pearl.

> One day when his court was assembled, King Mahmud placed a magnificent pearl in the hand of his vizier and asked him what it was worth.
>
> 'More than a hundred ass-loads of gold,' replied the vizier.
>
> 'Break it!' commanded the king.
>
> 'How could I break it when my greatest concern is the protection of your wealth?'
>
> 'Well answered!' exclaimed the king, and he rewarded the vizier with a fine robe.

The king gave the pearl to his chamberlain, asked him what it was worth, and then commanded him to break it. Like the vizier, the chamberlain refused and was rewarded with a fine robe and an increased salary. The king repeated the test one by one with the members of his entire court, who all replied as the vizier had done. The king rewarded them with money and robes, but in reality he was leading them from the Straight Path into the pit.

Eventually it was the turn of Ayaz. The king placed the pearl in his hand and asked him how much it was worth.

'More than I can say,' replied Ayaz.

'Break it!'

Ayaz, who had placed two stones up his sleeve, immediately crushed the pearl between them and reduced it to dust. The assembled courtiers gasped in disbelief, and cried out, 'What manner of recklessness is this? Only an infidel would break that radiant pearl!'

'O nobles, which is the more precious, the king's command or a pearl?' responded Ayaz.

The nobles bowed their heads in shame, but the king made a sign to his guards, as if to say, 'Remove these unworthy wretches from my presence, since they disobeyed my command for the sake of a stone.'

(M V: 4035–87)

Rumi tells the story of Ayaz's worn shoes and sheepskin jacket (the clothes he wore before he became the favourite of King Mahmud) to illustrate the *hadith*, 'Whoso knoweth himself knoweth his Lord.' Rumi also makes the point that we reveal ourselves through our actions. In the *Mathnawi*, the story extends over several pages and is interlaced with Rumi's commentary on the actions of Ayaz and his detractors. The version given here is abridged.

Ayaz was in the habit of withdrawing to a room to contemplate his old shoes and sheepskin jacket to remind himself of his humble origins. Some scheming courtiers, who assumed that Ayaz had a secret hoard of treasure, reported his actions to the king. The king ordered the Amir to open the door to the room at night, without Ayaz knowing. However, the king said to himself, 'Am I really giving this order? How upset Ayaz will be if he hears of this outrage! And yet I know that his loyalty to me is too great for him to be disturbed by my action.'

At midnight the Amir and his officers went to Ayaz's room. The door was heavily locked not because Ayaz had hoarded treasure but in order to keep his secret from mischievous eyes. When the officers burst into the room, all they found was a pair of worn shoes and a sheepskin jacket. 'These are a decoy,' they said. 'Bring pickaxes!' They dug up the floor and made holes in the walls, and wrought such devastation on the room that it was impossible to conceal what they had done. Shame-faced and covered in dust, they returned to the king.

The king asked the plotters, 'What has happened? Why have you come back empty-handed?'

When the plotters pleaded with the king to punish them or show them clemency, he insisted that the right to punish or pardon belonged to Ayaz. Ayaz replied, 'I know that I am nothing except those worn shoes and that sheepskin jacket. Everything else is your gift to me.'

This is the meaning of the *hadith*, 'Whoso knoweth himself knoweth his Lord.'

(M V: 1958–9, 1983–90, 2050–93, 2113–4)

Chapter Six

Rumi's Symbolism

Everything I say is an analogy . . . [for] those things that seem unintelligible become intelligible when they are expressed as analogies.

(F 44: A174/T173)

It is clear from Rumi's teachings and his understanding of the world that both duality and the notion of independent self-existence had passed away in his union with the Beloved. He was a living example of the Qur'anic verse, *Everything that exists will perish except His Face* (Q 28:88), for everywhere Rumi turned he saw nothing but the Face or Presence of God. The grinding sound of a millstone said to him, 'Glorious and Holy is He!'; the call of the stork (in Arabic, '*lak, lak*') was the soul calling out 'Thine is the kingdom'; on hearing a vendor of foxskins in the market at Konya shouting '*Dilku! Dilku!*' (Turkish for 'fox'), he broke into an ecstatic dance, calling out '*Dil ku? Dil ku?*' – which in Persian means 'Heart, where are you?' For Rumi, *whichever way you turn, there is the Face of God* (Q 2:115) was a living reality.

Also integral to Rumi's perception of the world in which we live is the Qur'anic verse *We belong to God, and to Him we are returning* (Q 2:156). As we saw in the story of Ayaz and the king's pearl (*see* page 135), the king's presents of money and fine robes diverted his courtiers from *the straight path* (Q 1:5) which, knowingly or unknowingly, we are all being guided along. How do we gain knowledge of this Path? Through knowing its opposite, *the path . . . of those who go astray* (Q 1:7). As we saw in the previous chapter, Rumi guides us onto the Straight Path through the interplay of opposites: Abraham and Nimrod, Moses and Pharaoh, Jesus and his ass, Ayaz and the king's courtiers.

A similar interplay is evident between the elements of Rumi's vast vocabulary of symbols. Some examples are explored in greater detail than others; and some are illustrated with a single quotation. To call them 'symbols' may be something of a misnomer; rather, they are examples of how Rumi saw the world around him – a world in which, to Rumi's eyes, *everything has perished except His Face* (Q 28:88).

THE MINERAL, PLANT AND ANIMAL REALMS

In Rumi's eyes, all creation is 'a great upward spiral of metamorphoses' (Lewis, *Rumi*, p. 416). In this upward, transformative spiral, the mineral realm becomes sustenance for plants, plants become food for animals, animals become food for humans, and humans have within them the potential to be transformed into a state in which they become one with the Divine Unity. Genuine transformation entails dying to one's present state, whatever that state might be, but as Rumi says in the following verses from the *Mathnawi* which encapsulate the transformative upward spiral of the creation, 'When did I ever become less by dying?'

> I died to the mineral realm and became a plant,
> I died to the plant realm and rose to the animal,
> I died to the animal realm and became human.
> What is there to fear?
> When did I ever become less by dying?
> In turn I'll die to my human form
> and soar on wings with the angels.
> But I must pass on even from the angel realm
> *for everything will perish except His Face* [Q 28:88].
> When my angel form is sacrificed
> I'll become what lies beyond the realms of imagination –
> non-existent!
> For Non-existence resonates within me,
> like the deep notes of an organ, saying
> *Verily, to Him we shall return* [Q 2:156]

(M III: 3901–6)

The potential that lies within every thing to be transformed to a higher state of being is reflected in the imagery drawn by Rumi from the different realms: mineral, plant, animal, human and the angelic. This imagery also reflects the potential for things to remain in their untransformed state or, in the case of human beings, to regress to a lower state of being.

The mineral realm

According to both biblical and Qur'anic tradition, Adam (humankind) was created from a mixture of clay (or earth) and water, and became a living being when God breathed His Spirit into him. Water and clay therefore represent our lowest level of being. When mined, however, dull earth offers up precious stones and gold. Likewise, if we mine our inner world, it too offers up precious stones – carnelians and rubies – and gold.

CLAY

> O world of water and clay,
> ever since I first knew you
> I've known but trial and pain.

> (D 1585: A1/195)

> Adam [humankind] was made from clay,
> but how does he resemble clay?

> (M V: 393)

PEARLS

> Behold the pearl of the soul in the oyster shell of the
> body . . .

> (D 621: from Arberry A1/77)

RUBIES

> A stone transformed into a flawless ruby
> becomes filled with the qualities of the sun.

(M V: 2025)

> The springtime of lovers has come,
> so this dustbowl may become a garden;
> the call from heaven has come,
> so the bird of the soul may take flight.
> The sea becomes filled with pearls,
> the salt marsh becomes as sweet as the waters of
>   Kauthar,
> the stone becomes a ruby from the mine
> the body becomes wholly soul.

(D536: after Arberry A I / 65)

GOLD

> The world is full of gold-diggers,
> but your self is where gold is mined.
> The Prophet said, 'Men are as mines';
> the self is a mine of silver and gold,
> and filled with precious gems.

(D 409: A I:48)

The plant realm

The transition from the mineral to the plant realm is captured in the second of the above quotations about rubies: spring comes and the 'dustbowl' of inanimate winter earth sprouts new life and is transformed into a garden. This seasonal transformation is a favourite analogy for Rumi since it equates with the quickening of the spirit within the water and clay of the human body. In Persian and Islamic literature, the finest of gardens is the rose garden, a synonym for Paradise. But even the rose garden presents us with a choice, for we can see it either as filled with thorns or with the beauty and scent of the rose, the universal symbol of Love.

THORNS

> If you think of roses, you are a rose-garden;
> if you think of thorns, you are fuel for the fire.

> (M II: 278)

> If you look for thorns when you enter Paradise,
> the only thorn you'll find is yourself.

> (M II: 3348)

THE ROSE

> He who turns fire into trees and roses is able to make this
>   world free from harm.
> He who brings forth roses from among thorns is able to
>   make winter turn to spring.

> (M VI: 1740–1)

> I am like the rose-garden of Paradise,
> I am a garden of joy in the world,
> for my spirit flows through the spirits of all people.

> (D 1615: A1/199)

> That which God said to the rose,
> and caused it to laugh in full-blown beauty,
> He said to my heart,
> and made it a hundred times more beautiful.

> (M III: 4129)

The animal kingdom

The upward spiral of our potential spiritual evolution has brought us to the animal kingdom. Here again, we are faced with the choice between either evolving to the next stage in the spiral and becoming fully human, or remaining subject to the whims and desires of our 'animal' or 'carnal' self. This choice extends to the way in which we view the realm of the plants. For the ass, plants are simply fodder; for the seeker of Truth, the plant realm – especially the rose – is a mirror that reflects the Beauty of God. Compared with the previous realms, the similarities in the behaviour of animals and humans provide Rumi with an enriched vocabulary of analogies. This is reflected in the increased length of some of the examples offered in this section.

THE ASS OR DONKEY

The words *ass*, *donkey* or *mule* are part of our everyday vocabulary – for example, 'Don't be an ass!' or 'You're as stubborn as a mule'. In Rumi's vocabulary, the same words are employed to denote stupid or stubborn behaviour. More significantly, when our lower nature is dominant we tend to be governed by its desires and impulses rather than by our higher nature. Rumi describes this tug-of-war between our lower and higher natures with a telling analogy in a discourse from *Fihi mafihi*:

> The human predicament can be likened to an angel's wing tied onto an ass's tail in the hope that the ass, through its association with the angel and the angelic light, might also become an angel.

> (F 25: A118/T111)

Our potential to rise above our ass-like lower nature lies in our capacity to attain knowledge of the Divine. This knowledge, which itself emanates from the Divine, is variously named as Intellect, Reason or Intelligence. Rumi continues his discourse on our human predicament with the following verse by Sana'i, the twelfth-century Persian Sufi poet.

Intellect gave Jesus wings
and he flew up into the heavens.
If his donkey had half a wing,
it would not have remained a donkey.

(F25: A118/T111–12)

Although our higher nature has the potential to draw us towards
higher levels of being, as long as we allow ourselves to be dominated
by our lower nature we cannot expect to evolve spiritually. Likening
our situation to that of a stubborn ass, Rumi expands on the wilfulness
of our lower nature:

> Idleness, greed and self-centredness have caused you to
> behave in a headstrong manner and to put your lower self
> in charge. You are like the ass that flees from its burden and
> heads for the mountains. Its master runs after it, calling out,
> 'Be warned, you stupid creature! If you disappear from my
> sight, wolves will come at you from every direction and
> devour you. Don't run away from me and the burden you
> have to carry, for I am your higher self. You are an ass and
> a beast of burden because you are controlled by your
> lower nature. O self-centred creature, don't you know that
> the dominant quality determines the nature of a thing? God
> intended you to behave like a horse and not an ass, for a
> horse responds to the command "*ta'al*" ("come"). Mustafa
> [Muhammad] was put in charge of the stableyard for your
> animal nature. Out of compassion, God said to him, "*Say,
> 'ta'alaw (come ye)* [Q 3:57], so that I may train you, for I am
> the trainer'."

(M IV: 1996–2006)

Continuing with the equestrian analogy, Rumi goes on to explain that
each self has its own individual stable, and so we respond to the call
ta'alaw in different ways. Some are deaf to it. Others are frightened by
it. Yet the Divine Word *ta'alaw* is a powerful elixir and not to be

underestimated. If we turn away from it, it will not be withheld from us. If our lower self currently holds us in its spell, we may benefit from the Word later on. 'O slave of God, *say, Ta'alaw, ta'alaw (Come ye, come ye)*. Come back from your headstrong, self-centred ways.' If our lower nature runs amuck, Rumi tells us to take it firmly in hand, 'If an ass goes mad, beat it over the head with a bull-whip until it comes back to its senses' (D 304).

We leave the last word on the lower self and its symbolic pairing with the much-maligned ass to Rumi, although strictly speaking it is through practical demonstration rather than words that he reinforces the pairing while making a necessary distinction between the animal and our animal nature. Aflaki relates that:

> One day Jalaluddin set out on an ass for the country home of Husamuddin. Along the way, he observed, 'This is the beast ridden by the righteous. Several of the prophets have ridden on asses: Seth, Ezra, Jesus, and Muhammad.'
>
> It so happened that one of his disciples was also mounted on an ass. The beast suddenly began to bray loudly, much to the annoyance of its rider who began to beat the ass over the head.
>
> Jalaluddin remonstrated with his disciple, saying, 'Why beat the poor creature? Are you beating him because he is carrying your burden? Are you not grateful that you are the rider and he the vehicle? Let's suppose that, God forbid, the situation were reversed. What would you do? His braying comes from one of two things: his stomach or his lust. In this he is like all other creatures. They are all constantly motivated by either the desire for food or their earthly passions. All of them, therefore, would have to be chastised and beaten over the head.'
>
> The shamed disciple dismounted, kissed the hoof of his ass, and stroked his head.
>
> (Aflaki, *Legends of the Sufis*, pp. 37–8)

THE DOG

> How would a person who, like a dog, is attached by its
> nature to its kennel [the world], have a desire for
> spiritual lordship?'

(M V: 831)

THE PORCUPINE

Rumi likens the soul of the believer to the porcupine: when you beat
it, it spreads out its quills and grows bigger.

> There is an animal called the porcupine that grows big and
> fat when beaten with a stick.
> The more you beat it, the more it thrives: it grows stout
> on the blows of a stick.
> The true believer's soul is a porcupine, for it grows stout
> on the blows of suffering.
> This is why the suffering of the prophets and saints is
> greater than that of any other creature.

(M IV: 97–100)

THE MOUSE

This timid little creature scuttles out of sight the moment it senses
danger, and so it embodies the aspect of the human self that behaves
in a similar way. According to Rumi, 'They [the lesser and Greater Holy
Wars] are not the work of those whose reason and intellect jump from
his body at the twitch of a mouse's tail' (M V: 3802). The following
story of the mouse and the camel suggests that the mouse can even
become the tail that wags the dog, so to speak, thus hampering our
spiritual evolution.

> A mouse caught hold of a camel's lead-rope with his
> forelegs, and, imitating what it had seen others do, walked
> off with it. Because the camel readily followed him, the
> mouse thought himself something of a hero. Sensing what

the mouse was thinking, the camel said to himself, 'I'll show you what's what later. Enjoy for now your moment of glory!'

They continued in this way until they came to the edge of a river that was so wide it would have intimidated the bravest of creatures. The mouse stopped, paralysed with fear. 'Why have you stopped?' asked the camel. 'You are the one leading me. Don't give up halfway. Be a man and cross the river!'

'The river is vast,' said the mouse. 'I'm afraid of drowning!'

The camel stepped forward into the water, saying, 'Let me see how deep it is. Look, it's only knee-deep. Why did you lose your nerve?'

'It may only be as deep as your knee,' replied the mouse, 'but it's a hundred times deeper than the top of my head.'

'Next time,' said the camel, 'don't behave so rashly. Grapple with someone your own size, for a mouse has nothing to say to a camel.'

'I repent. Please get me across this deadly river,' pleaded the mouse.

Taking pity on him, the camel said, 'Jump up onto my hump, since it has been granted me to cross the river. I could take thousands like you.'

(M II: 3436–52)

THE CAMEL

For the countries of the Middle and Near East, the camel was a mode of transport as indispensable as the motor car is for us in the West today. Like most things that are an integral part of everyday life, the camel took on a symbolic value of its own, notably as a 'vehicle' for the spiritual journey. But as an often repeated *hadith* instructs us, 'Trust in God, but first tether your camel!' In contrast to the ass, that other mode of animal transport, the camel is of a superior kind, as illustrated in the following abridged version of Rumi's anecdote.

A camel, an ox and a ram were travelling down a road together when they came across a tuft of fresh grass. The ram said, 'If we divide this between us, none of us will eat his fill. It should fall to the eldest of us to eat it, for did not the Prophet tell us to honour our elders. Let us settle the matter by each declaring our age. For myself, I once shared a pasture with the ram that Abraham sacrificed in place of Ishmael.'

'I am the oldest,' said the ox, 'for I was one of the oxen yoked to the plough with which Adam, the forefather of mankind, tilled the soil.'

The camel listened to his companions in stunned silence. Then, lowering his long neck, he plucked that delicious tuft of barley grass and, without any further ado, raised the grass in the air and ate it. As he did so, he said to his companions, 'I have no need of chronology, since every one knows, my dears, that I am taller than you. Any intelligent person knows that I am by nature superior to you both.'

(M VI: 2457–83)

Rumi makes a distinction between the human intellect – our faculty for discernment – which is described as 'partial intellect', and the Universal Intellect (*see* 'Two kinds of intelligence', page 167). The intellect paves the way for Love; but if we allow our ego to limit our intellect in any way, there will be no room for Love to enter.

If you build a coop for your hen,
A camel will not fit inside – its neck is too long!
The hen is the intellect; the coop is your body;
The camel is Love, most glorious and high.

(D 2937: after Schimmel, *Rumi's World*, p. 189)

My soul runs after Thee like a drunken camel;
My body is a halter bound around the camel's neck.

(D 2331: A2:297)

Majnun and his she-camel

Rumi relates a story about Majnun and his she-camel to illustrate the tug-of-war between the heart and the body: the heart wishes to rejoin the Beloved (represented here by Layla), while the body (the she-camel) wants to go in the opposite direction. The story is told in both the *Mathnawi* and *Fihi mafihi*, and the version given here is an amalgamation of the two.

> Majnun desired to rejoin his beloved Layla, but his she-camel's desire was to run back to its foal. So long as he was fully awake, he rode in that direction. But if he forgot himself for even a moment, the camel would feel the rein slacken and, sensing his distraction, would turn on its tracks and head back towards her foal. This happened often, for Majnun was frequently lost in thoughts of Layla. When he came to his senses, he would find that he had travelled for two days in the opposite direction. He thus continued to go backward and forward for many years on a journey that would normally have taken three days. Finally he said, 'O camel, we are both lovers but we make unsuitable travelling companions. The object of your affections is not the same as mine, we must therefore go our separate ways. You are enamoured of your home and, so long as you are with me, my soul remains far from Layla. Union with my beloved lies only a short distance away, but because of your noose around my neck I have been travelling for sixty years! I am sick of riding. Sick, sick, sick!" So saying, he jumped off the camel and went his way on foot, singing: 'My camel's desire is behind me, and my desire lies ahead. Truly, she and I could not agree.'

> (M IV: 1534–59; F 4: A29/T18)

Soul birds

Birds are an essential element in Rumi's vocabulary. For centuries before Rumi's time, the bird had lent itself as a symbol for the human soul. Bird-like, the soul can either fly free, winging its way to the heavens, or it can remain here on Earth, imprisoned in the cage of the body. The mannerisms of birds, too, can mirror human qualities: one can strut like a peacock, crow like a rooster, fuss like a mother-hen, be eagle-eyed, or parrot the actions of others. Some human qualities are considered useful, others not. For Rumi, there are four particular qualities that are detrimental to our progress along the Path. These four qualities are the subject of a commentary on a passage from the Qur'an, in which Abraham (Khalil) has asked God to show him how He brings the dead to life, and God replies, *Take four birds and train them to turn to you* (Q 2:260). Rumi continues:

> O you who are the Khalil of the age, kill these four birds that beset the Way, since, crow-like, they pluck out the eye of the intellect of the intelligent. Human beings harbour four heart-oppressing qualities that resemble Khalil's four birds: slaughtering them in the name of God allows the soul to ascend . . . Since the body is where these four qualities nest, they are called the four mischief-makers. If you want human beings to attain to eternal life, then cut off the heads of these four loathsome and evil birds, and then bring them back to life, transformed into another sort, so that afterwards they will do no harm. The four formless birds that beset the Way have made their nest in the hearts of human beings . . . These are the duck, the peacock, the crow, and the rooster: they are allegories for the four pernicious qualities in human beings. The duck is greed, the rooster is lust, the peacock is superiority, and the crow is worldly desire.'
>
> (M V: 31–3, 37–40, 43–4)

In the verses that follow, Rumi contrasts the negative qualities associated with these birds with the actions of the true believer. However, the meaning Rumi attributes to some birds is ambivalent, changing from one context to the next, depending on the point he is making. In one context, the rooster is lust; in another, Rumi hears him calling believers to their early morning prayers, and asks himself if 'this useful creature is not in reality an *angelos* . . . rather than an ordinary bird?' (Schimmel, *Rumi's World*, p. 70) While the duck may embody greed, in another context she is likened to the human soul: since she is equally at home on earth and water, she is able – if she follows her true nature – to leave dry land behind her and swim in the Ocean of spiritual reality. (M II: 3722).

Birdsong, too, echoes the state of the human soul, from the raucous 'caw' of the crow to the nightingale's song of love for the rose. The calls of certain birds become puns for Rumi, the multi-linguist. The dove's 'coo, coo' is the call of the seeker, for in Persian *ku ku* means 'Where, where?' In Arabic, the *'lak lak'* of the stork is the soul crying out, 'Thine is the kingdom' (M II: 1661–2). Even the egg has lessons to teach us:

> This world and that world are the egg,
> and the bird within is in darkness,
> broken-winged, and reviled.
> Consider unbelief and faith
> as the white and yolk of the egg,
> at once joined and divided
> by *a barrier they shall not pass.*
> When He nurses the egg under His wing,
> unbelief and religion disappear,
> and the bird Unity takes to the air.

> (after Nicholson, *Selected Poems
> from the Divana Shamsi Tabriz*, p. 221)

> Ritual prayer is like an egg, so hatch the chick!
> Don't just bob aimlessly up and down.

> (M III: 2175)

As for the birds themselves, they can be loosely divided into two kinds: those that represent the spiritually blind or the human being within whom the spirit lies dormant; and those that symbolize the lover, yearning to be reunited with the Beloved. In the latter category, the falcon and the nightingale reign supreme.

THE CROW OR RAVEN

These two birds share a similar symbolic meaning in that both are associated with death and graveyards. The Qur'an relates how a raven showed Cain how to bury Abel after he had murdered him. *Then Allah sent a raven, who scratched up the ground, to show him [Cain] how to hide his brother's naked corpse. 'Woe is me!' he cried, 'am I not even able to be as this raven, and so hide my brother's naked corpse?' And he repented* (Q 5:31). Rumi retells this incident in both *Fihi mafihi* (F 38: A152/T149) and the *Mathnawi* (M IV: 1301ff.) to illustrate the shortcomings of the partial intellect. In both these versions, the bird kills one of its kind and then digs a grave to bury it in, thus instructing Cain how to bury his brother. In *Fihi mafihi*, Rumi comments, 'Everyone possessing partial intellect is in need of instruction, and the Universal Intellect is the originator of all things. Those who have united the partial intellect with the Universal Intellect so that they become one are the saints and prophets.' Rumi's lengthier commentary accompanying the version in the *Mathnawi* is as follows:

> Concerning the Universal Intellect, He [God] said,
> 'The sight did not rove,' but the partial intellect looks in
> every direction.
> The Intellect whose sight does not rove is the light
> of the saints. The crow-intellect is the grave-digger for
> the spiritually dead.
> The spirit that flies after the crow is led by the
> crow towards the graveyard.
> Beware! Do not follow the crow-like bodily soul,
> for it takes you to the graveyard, not towards the orchard.
>
> (M IV: 1309–12)

When Solomon speaks to the birds, the hoopoe claims to possess the 'eye of certainty'. Envious of the hoopoe's spiritual station, the crow launches a verbal attack on him, accusing him of lying. Speaking in his own defence, the hoopoe says, 'The crow denies the authority of the Divine decree, so he is an unbeliever, even though his intellect is great.' (M I: 1229.)

Yet the crow is not quite the bird of death it seems to be. As a member of the flock of birds enlightened by Solomon, 'although it had the form of a crow, inwardly it aspired to be a falcon.' (M II: 3752.)

THE OWL

A bird of the night, the owl is associated with darkness and spiritual death. But whereas the crow and raven frequent the graveyard, the owl dwells among ruins. However, it shares a common characteristic with those big black birds in that it attacks the spiritual falcon.

> Like blind and clumsy birds are we,
> for we ignore the spiritual Solomon.
> Like the owls, we have become hostile to the falcon,
> and so we are condemned to dwell in ruins.

> (M II: 3746–7)

THE DUCK

In an earlier passage from the *Mathnawi*, Rumi associated the duck with greed. Here he presents us with a different image:

> Your birth-mother was a duck, but your wet-nurse was a
>   domesticated chicken.
> Your true mother was an Ocean-going bird; your earth-
>   bound foster mother was at home on dry land.
> The call of the Ocean you feel in your soul comes from
>   your natural mother.
> Your desire to remain on dry land comes from your wet-
>   nurse. Leave your nurse – she's a bad influence.
> Leave her on dry land. It's time to rejoin the spiritual
>   Ocean, and swim with the other ducks.
> If you are told that the water is dangerous, don't be

afraid. Press on until you reach the Ocean.
Ducks are at home on both land and water, whereas
   chickens are cooped up in stinking henhouses.

(M II: 3766–72)

THE PARROT

The parrot is renowned for its capacity to imitate the human voice.
Rumi tells the following story about a parrot that gained its freedom by
imitating the behaviour of another.

A certain merchant kept a parrot in a cage. When he was
preparing to travel to India on business, he asked the
parrot if there was anything he could bring back for it. The
parrot replied, 'When you see the parrots in India, tell
them that you have a parrot who lives in a cage and to think
of her as they fly freely over the fields.'

When the merchant arrived in India, he stopped by a
field full of parrots and delivered his parrot's message. On
hearing the message, one of the birds immediately fell
down and died. 'Oh, dear,' said the merchant, with regret.
'That parrot must have been related to mine, like two
bodies sharing the same spirit. Why didn't I keep my mouth
shut? Now my words have killed that poor bird.'

Having finished his business, the merchant returned
home and said to his parrot, 'I delivered your message to
some parrots that looked just like you. When they heard of
your predicament, one of them immediately dropped
down dead. I regretted what I'd said, but what use were
regrets?'

On hearing what the other parrot had done, the
merchant's parrot fell to the floor of her cage. Mourning his
dead parrot, the merchant picked her up and took her out
of the cage. The dead bird immediately came to life and
flew off. From the safety of a tree, she explained to the
merchant that the Indian parrot had sent her a message,
'Become dead like me, so that you may gain your freedom.'

The parrot gave him further spiritual advice, after which the merchant said to her, 'May God protect you, for you have shown me a new path.' When the parrot had flown away, he said to himself, 'Is my soul any less than the parrot? I will follow her example and take the path of freedom.'

(abridged from M I: 1547–1845)

THE NIGHTINGALE

Of all the soul-birds, the nightingale is perhaps the most evocative because of its close association with the rose. For the Persian poets, this association stems from the return of the nightingale in the spring, the season when roses come into bloom. The bird's melodious and prolific song, which heralds the transition from winter to spring, is attributed to its reunion with its beloved rose. It is the beauty of the rose that causes the nightingale to return, and so the nightingale and the rose personify the return of the lover to the Beloved.

The nightingale said to the rose,
'Tell me, what is in your heart?
Tell me now, for no one else is here;
only you and I.'
The rose replied, 'Don't even think of this
so long as you are with yourself.
Try to lift the burden of selfhood
out of this world of water and clay.'

(D 45: A1:6)

When you see a confidant, tell him of spiritual mysteries,
and when you see a rose, sing like a nightingale.

(M VI: 2037)

THE FALCON

Rumi leaves us in no doubt as to the symbolic significance of the falcon, for he tells us that 'the spirit is a falcon' (M V: 843), and that it is 'wholly light, emanating from the Light of Divine Grace' (M II: 1133). Since the falcon-spirit returns to its place on the wrist of the king when the falcon-drum sounds the call, *Return!* (M II: 1169), it is also the embodiment of the Qur'anic verse *To God we belong, and to Him we return* (Q 2:156). But only those who return to the king's wrist are worthy of the name falcon. Those who lose their way are blind falcons, like the bird in Rumi's story that found itself in the wilderness (the world), living among owls (worldly people).

> Destiny threw dust in the falcon's eyes and left it in the wilderness, among owls and far from the Path. The owls attacked the falcon and tore out its regal plumage. Protesting loudly at the presence of their uninvited visitor, they exclaimed, 'The falcon has come to steal our home!'
>
> 'Why should I seek the company of owls?' asked the falcon. 'I leave a hundred wildernesses like this one to the owls. Don't get so agitated, for I'm not staying here. This ruin may be your idea of home, but for me the King's wrist is the place to return to.'
>
> 'Don't listen to him!' warned the ringleader of the owls. 'The falcon is plotting to turn you out of your home. He cunningly boasts about the King and the King's wrist in order to divert us simple folk. Anyone who believes what he says is a fool. How can a small bird like this be the friend of royalty?
>
> (M II: 1131)

In the *Mathnawi*, Rumi tells the story of a falcon that fled from the king and was caught by an old woman (the world), who clipped its wings, cut its talons and fed it on straw. The king went in search of the falcon, and when he found it in this sorry state, he told the falcon that this is what happens when one flees from the king to the house of an old hag. The king asked the falcon, 'Why would you want to make your home in Hell when you have lived in Paradise?' The falcon repented, rubbing what was left of its wings against the king's wrist (M II: 323–34).

The spirit is a falcon; human attributes are crows.
The falcon suffers many wounds from crows and owls.

(M V: 843)

The human realm

Having ascended the evolutionary path through the realms of
minerals, plants and animals, we come to the human realm. In the eyes
of our ego, our evolutionary path does not progress beyond this realm
and so this is where it wishes to remain. It thus sets itself at odds with
our soul, whose purpose is to continue. Rumi sums up our
predicament as being that of 'an angel's wing tied onto an ass's tail' –
one part of us wishes to ascend to a higher state of being, the other
wishes to descend to a lower. In effect, we find ourselves with a choice
between the two paths alluded to in the opening surah of the Qur'an,
the straight path and *the path of those who go astray* (Q 1:6, 7). Rumi
leaves us in no doubt as to what makes us hesitate in our choice.

THE WORLD

The world is a trap, and desire is its bait: escape
the traps and quickly turn your face toward God.
When you have followed the Path, you have
enjoyed a hundred blessings; when you have taken
another path, you have fared badly.
So the Prophet said, 'Consult your own hearts,
even though the religious lawyer advises you on worldly
affairs.'
Abandon desire, so that you may receive His
Mercy: you know from experience that this is what He
requires.
Since you have no way of escape, be His servant,
and go from His prison into His rose-garden.

(M VI: 377–82)

At times, the world is likened to a seductive enchantress or an old hag.

> Do you know, brother, that you are a son of Adam, a
> prince newly born into an old world? The world is like the
> witch of Kabul, who held human beings prisoner with her
> colour and perfume. To free yourself from this witchcraft,
> repeat without ceasing the words, *I take refuge with the Lord*
> *of the daybreak.*
>   The Prophet likened this world to an enchantress, for
> her spells keep humankind dwelling in the pit of perdition.
> Beware! The stinking old hag has powerful spells: her hot
> breath has enslaved kings. This sorceress world is an
> extremely cunning woman: her sorcery cannot be undone by
> the ignorant. If human beings knew how to loosen her bonds,
> why would God have sent the prophets? Listen, seek out one
> whose breath is cool, who can loosen the bonds, and who
> knows the mystery of *God doeth whatsoever He wills.*
>
> (M IV: 3189–99)

A few verses later, Rumi presents us with a very different vision of the
world.

> The entire universe is the form of Universal
> Reason, which is the father of whoever is a follower of
> the Divine Word.
>   When a person shows ingratitude to Universal
> Reason, the universe takes on the appearance of a rabid
> dog.
>   Make your peace with this Father, abandon
> disobedience, so that the water and clay of the world may
> become a carpet of gold . . .
>   Since I am always at peace with this Father, this
> world is Paradise to my eyes.
>   At every moment fresh forms and new beauty
> appear . . .
>
> (M IV: 3259–61, 3263–4)

MEN AND WOMEN

Intellect and ego

From the perspective of our modern age, the role sometimes assigned to women in Rumi's writings is open to misunderstanding and misinterpretation. Where we may be gender-sensitive, Rumi is not. For Rumi, the interaction between the men and women who people his writings is essentially the interplay of the archetypal active/passive polarities found in most metaphysical or esoteric traditions – such as the yang and yin of Taoism. Rumi is quite clear about this when he says:

> In the view of the intellect, heaven is the man and
> the earth the woman: whatever the one throws down, the
> other nurtures.
> When the earth lacks warmth, heaven sends it
> down; when the earth lacks freshness and moisture,
> heaven bestows it . . .
> The heavens turn in the world of time, just as men
> turn in their search to sustain their wife.
> The earth is like a housewife: it brings forth life
> and nurtures what it brings forth.
> Therefore look on heaven and earth as being
> endowed with intelligence, for they function like
> intelligent beings . . .
> The desire for the male was implanted in the
> female so that the two may perfect each other's work.
> God implanted desire in man and woman so that
> the world would be sustained by their union.

> (M III: 4404–5, 4409–11, 4414–15)

While the last two verses may be understood as a reference to the male and female genders, alternatively they may be understood as expressing the ideal relationship between the intellect and the ego. As William Chittick explains:

In the human microcosm, the Universal Intellect and the
Universal Soul are reflected in the intellect and the ego.
However, because of [humankind's] unique position
among creatures, the natural order of things is sometimes
distorted or even reversed. In other words, the intellect
should be active in relation to the passive ego. The intellect
should discern truth from falsehood like a sword and then
make decisions upon the basis of this discernment; and the
ego should animate and control the body in keeping with
the intellect's directives . . . If [humankind] were to rejoin
[its] primordial perfection, [its] intellect would once again
play a masculine role, and [its] ego would live in harmony
with it as its feminine mate.

  If duality were to leave our heart and spirit for a moment,
  our intellect would be Adam, our ego Eve. (D 2447)

(Chittick, *The Sufi Path of Love*, pp. 163–4)

In this same spirit, Rumi employs the terms 'hermaphrodite' and
'pederast' to illustrate the imbalance between the archetypal
masculine and feminine principles embodied in the intellect and the
ego (*see* the story of the Pear Tree, page 209).

Man

For Rumi, 'man', 'manhood' and 'manliness' are terms that can be
applied equally to men and women to denote a person who has
attained a state of spiritual maturity.

  A child demands walnuts and raisins, but these are mere
    trifles for a man of intellect.
  To the eye of the heart, the body is walnuts and raisins –
    so how will a child gain the knowledge of men?
  Whoever is veiled from God is in fact a child: a *man* has
    passed beyond doubt.
  If you consider yourself a man because of your beard and
    testicles, any he-goat has plenty of hair and a beard.

(M V: 3342–5)

Woman

Many Westerners take exception to the apparent subordination of women in Islamic cultures. However, this subordination may arise from the literal interpretation of a *hadith* of the Prophet, who said, 'Put the women last!' As Rumi explains:

> When the Prophet said, 'Put the women last!', he meant
>   your ego. For it must be put last, and your intellect
>   first.

(M II: 1856)

The subordination of women is also the subject of Rumi's commentary on the *hadith*, 'They [women] hold dominion over the wise man, but the ignorant man holds dominion over them.'

> The Prophet said that women have the upper hand
> over the wise and intelligent man,
>   but that fools have the upper hand over women
> because they are slaves to their animal nature.
>   They have no tenderness, kindness or affection,
> because their animal nature has the upper hand over their
> human nature.
>   Love and tenderness are human qualities, anger
> and lust are animal qualities.
>   Woman is a ray of God, she is not a mere mistress.
> She is the Creator's self. One might even say, she is not
> created!

(M I: 2433–7)

Chapter Seven

Themes from Rumi

This present world is but a dream; the sleeper imagines
it to be real.

(M IV: 3654)

The range of Rumi's thematic imagery is vast. In addition to the
characters and symbols explored in the preceding chapters, his
metaphors and analogies are drawn from the world of everyday
experience. The changing seasons, especially the transition from
winter to spring, become a metaphor for our spiritual awakening. The
kitchen is equated with the world, cooking with our spiritual
evolution, and food is either food for the sensual self or food for the
heart. The ocean is the Divine Unity, while the drop of water is the
human individual drawn inexorably towards the Source of his/her
being.

Beneath these themes lie two other themes central to Rumi's
teaching. The first, which permeates Rumi's references to the world of
everyday experience, is an affirmation of the Divine Unity in that
Wheresoever you turn, there is His Face [or *Presence*] (Q 2:115). But
recognition of, and awakening to, the Divine Unity is merely the first
step on our path, the second step is expressed in another theme –
sometimes implicit, sometimes overtly stated – namely, *We belong to
God, and unto Him we are returning* (Q 2:156). These two themes are
also expressed in terms of 'being' and 'non-being', or 'existence' and
'non-existence', for in awakening to the fact that the Divine Unity is *all*
that exists, we realize that no 'thing', including ourselves, exists
independently of It. In this sense, the self we perceive as 'me' is deemed
to be non-existent, an illusory reality. Our sense of self-existence is so

strong, however, that the idea of self-annihilation (*fana'*) is one of our greatest fears. Hence the Sufis' frequent reference to the *hadith*, 'Die before you die.' But before we can take such a step, we need to understand something about our nature as human beings: why we are what we are, and why we do the things we do. This chapter explores variations on this theme.

THE NATURE OF HUMAN BEING

In the Fourth Discourse in *Fihi mafihi*, Rumi tells us that we come into the world for a specific purpose but that our desire to do other, more mundane things, diverts us from fulfilling this purpose. He likens our situation to a priceless sword being used to cut up offal, a jewel-encrusted dagger being used as a nail from which to hang a broken gourd, or a golden bowl being used to cook turnips (*see* page 191). In short, we are unaware of our true nature as human beings. Rumi seeks to rectify this in the following passages from *Fihi mafihi* and the *Mathnawi*, in which he describes three kinds of creature and two kinds of intelligence.

Three kinds of creature

Discourse Seventeen in *Fihi mafihi* begins with a member of Rumi's audience observing that there seems to be little difference between unbelievers and those who consider themselves Muslims. In the past, unbelievers worshipped idols and (in Rumi's own time) Muslims are doing the selfsame thing in that they bow externally to the Mongols, and bow internally to other idols, such as greed, lust, anger and envy. Rumi responds by saying that since not everyone is able to see by the light of faith implanted in them by God, some people are happy to remain in their existing state, however hideous it might appear to others. To them, it seems perfectly natural. Rumi explains that this state of affairs arises because 'God will grant you whatever you desire in your heart. Whatever you aspire to will be granted you, for as the saying goes, "A bird flies by means of its wings; a believer flies by means of his aspiration".' (F 17: A89/T81.) He continues his discourse with a

commentary on the following *hadith* of the Prophet, according to
which creatures can be divided into three kinds: 'God created the
angels and placed within them the intellect, and He created the beasts
and placed within them sensuality, and He created the children of
Adam and placed within them both intellect and sensuality. So the one
whose intellect prevails over his sensuality is higher than the angels,
and the one whose sensuality prevails over his intellect is lower than
the beasts.' Rumi includes a similar commentary on this *hadith* in the
Mathnawi (M IV 1497–1532). The version given here combines the
essence of both passages.

> There are three kinds of creatures. First are the angels,
> who are pure intelligence. It is their nature to be constantly
> mindful of God, to worship and obey Him. This is what
> sustains them. It is both their food and their means of life.
> In this they are like a fish who lives in water, whose life
> comes from the water, and whose bed and pillow are the
> water. Angels are under no obligation to do what they do.
> They are pure light and free from lust, so they do not have
> to struggle with sensual passions. Their obedience to God
> is not regarded as obedience, for it is in their nature and
> they cannot be otherwise.
>
> The second kind are the beasts, who are pure lust and
> lacking in intelligence. They are like an animal grown fat
> from eating, who sees nothing but its stable and its fodder.
> They too are under no obligation to do what they do.
>
> The third kind are human beings, the descendants of
> Adam, who are a combination of intelligence and lust. They
> are half-angel, half-ass; half-serpent, half-fish. Their ass-half
> draws them toward whatever is low; their angelic-half
> draws them toward the light. Their fish-half draws them
> toward the water, their serpent-half draws them toward
> the earth. Angels and beasts are free of conflict and
> struggle – the angels because of their knowledge, the
> beasts because of their ignorance – and between the two
> lies the human being whose lot is to endure a constant tug-
> of-war. 'He whose intellect overcomes his lust is higher

than the angels; he whose lust overcomes his intellect is lower than the beasts.'

Moreover, through the trials it has undergone, the human race has been divided. Although they all have human form, in reality human beings have developed into three communities. Those in the first group have become completely submerged [in the Ocean] and, like Jesus, have become totally angelic and pure light. These are the prophets and the saints. Their form is that of Adam, but their essence is Gabriel. They are free of fear and hope, anger, sensual passion, and argument. They are also free of discipline, asceticism, and self-mortification. It is as though they were not even born of the children of Adam.

The second group comprises those whose intellects have been so overcome by their lust that they have become totally bestial and taken on the nature of the ass. The qualities of Gabriel were in them once, but these have flown. Whoever is bereft of spirit is [spiritually] dead; when his spirit is bereft of angelic qualities, he becomes an ass. Yet he suffers more anxiety than the beasts, for the cunning and fraudulent deception which he spins is not produced by any other animal. Weaving gold-embroidered robes, taking pearls from the seabed, the arts of geometry and astronomy, and the sciences of medicine and philosophy are all connected with this world, and do not bring us any nearer to the seventh heaven. These things build a worldly stable for the ox and the camel, but in order to harbour their animal nature for a while longer these imbeciles describe them as 'mysteries'. Because of their animal nature, they know only the sleep of the ignorant, and their perception of reality is upside-down. They had the capacity for transformation, but they have lost it. They are the lowest of the low. Avoid them.

There remains the third group. These are the people engaged in the struggle between their animal and angelic natures. They experience a degree of anguish and distress, and are not content with their current way of life. These are the believers. The saints are waiting for them, to bring them to their own station and make them equal to themselves. The devils lie in wait for them too, to drag them down with them to the lowest of the low.

Rumi continues his commentary in the *Mathnawi*, illustrating the struggle between our higher and lower natures with an anecdote about Majnun and his she-camel (*see* page 150).

Two kinds of intelligence

There are two kinds of intelligence. The first is the one you acquire through learning, in the manner of schoolchildren, from books and teachers, from reflection and memorizing facts, from forming concepts and from the study of subjects that are new to you. In this way your intelligence surpasses that of others, but in reality the retention of all this knowledge in your mind is a burden. In your quest for knowledge you have become little more than a tablet on which one records information. Yet there is another kind of tablet, another form of intelligence. This other intelligence is the gift of God: it flows from within you, from the depths of your soul. Unlike the first kind of intelligence, the water of divine knowledge never stinks with stagnation. It doesn't matter if it is prevented from flowing into the outside world, for it pours forth from the heart in an unending flow. On the other hand, acquired intelligence is like the water supply entering a house from the outside: if it gets blocked, the house ends up without any water. So seek the fount of knowledge within you!

(M IV: 1960–8)

Having defined the two fundamental forms of intelligence in this way, Rumi proceeds to illustrate the difference between them with an account of the Prophet Muhammad's appointment of a young man from the tribe of Hudhayl as commander of one of his armies. In

Rumi's account, the Prophet is portrayed as the embodiment of divine knowledge. Acquired knowledge is represented by a man who objects to the appointment of a young man over men who are older, and therefore, in the objector's eyes, wiser than the appointee. Yet acquired knowledge is such that it is unaware of the superiority of divine knowledge, and this is conveyed by the Prophet remaining silent before the objector's unending flow of words. Moreover, to harangue the Prophet in this way not only demonstrated a total disregard for the Prophet's position as the Messenger of God, it also showed a similar disregard for his spiritual station. In this way Rumi uses the objector's dissent to comment on our unenlightened state, in which our desire for that which is transient (and therefore perishable) is the cause of our own perishing.

> In the presence of the Prophet, words poured forth in an unending flow from the irreverent objector's lips. But he was unaware that acquired knowledge is merely hearsay in the presence of divine insight. Indeed, hearsay is substituted for vision. As such, it is favoured by those who are absent and shunned by those who are present. For the visionary, hearsay is of no consequence. When you are in the presence of your beloved, you no longer need chaperones or go-betweens. Dismiss them! Whoever leaves his childhood behind and becomes a true man finds love-letters and go-betweens tediousness itself. Such a person reads letters in order to teach others; he speaks in order to increase their understanding. When you are in the presence of an enlightened person, indulging in hearsay is inappropriate for it reveals our ignorance and lack of true knowledge. In the presence of such a person, silence is the best policy. That is why we received the divine injunction, *Be silent* [Q 7:204].

> (M IV; 2064–72)

Later in the same account, Rumi likens the objector's conduct in the presence of the Prophet to someone who brings a bag of dried dung, saying, 'Have this instead of a musk-scented bag.' His lack of true intelligence leads him to hold a lump of camel dung under his nose and exclaim, 'What a delightful smell!' In his delusion, he thinks he is wiser than someone whose inner organ of smell is accustomed to the scent of the celestial rose-garden. As Rumi says, 'Silence is the Ocean, and speech is like the river. The Ocean is seeking you out; do not seek out the river' (M IV: 2062).

Rumi's reference to musk and camel dung, two self-evident opposites, illustrates the recurring theme that we get to know a thing through its opposite. Learning to see dung as dung, rather than imagining it to be sweet-smelling musk, is the beginning of our awakening to who we really are. For as Rumi says, what we see is what we are:

> You are not your body: you are the Eye. When you see the Spirit, you are free of the body.
> A human being is an eye; the rest is just flesh and bones. Whatever your eye sees, you are that.

> (M VI: 811–12)

But it is not only how we see what we see that reveals whether our inclination is towards material or spiritual reality. The company we keep – who we are drawn to, and who avoids us – also reveals our inner qualities.

> When two people keep company, they clearly have something in common.
> Would a bird fly with birds that are not of its own kind? . . .
> A wise man said, 'I was amazed to see a crow with a stork. So I set out to see what they had in common.
> Bewildered, I drew closer to them and saw that what they had in common was that both were lame.
> Why would a royal falcon, a bird of the highest heaven, seek out an owl, which is of the lowest earth?

> (M II: 2101–2, 2103–6)

A similar theme is illustrated by Rumi's tale of the man who was befriended by a bear (*see* page 205).

From duality to nonduality

'THINGS BECOME CLEAR THROUGH THEIR OPPOSITES'
The significance of the proverbial expression 'things become clear through their opposites', which is often quoted or alluded to by Rumi, is explained by William Chittick:

> . . . the existence of the myriad things of the world only becomes possible through differentiation and opposition. If two things were not different, and therefore 'opposed' in some respect, they would be one and the same. Each individual of a pair of opposites makes the existence of the other individual possible; day and night, perfection and imperfection, wholeness and brokenness, happiness and sadness, newness and oldness, spirit and body. Each of these correlative terms can only exist and be known because of its opposite. And so it is with all things, except God. He alone has no opposite, but transcends all opposition. He alone is the true 'coincidence of opposites' (*jam'-i addad*), where all opposition is effaced in the Ocean of Unity. For the same reason, we cannot know Him, since He has no opposite to 'make Him clear'.
>
> (Chittick, *The Sufi Path of Love*, p. 49)

This duality of opposites remains part of our everyday experience of the world until such time as our sense of 'self' dissolves, like a drop of water, in the Ocean of Unity. In the meantime, we can utilize our experience of the duality of everyday life to learn to discern what is food for the lower self and what is food for our heart or soul. Rumi helps us in this by constantly drawing our attention to the world of opposites so that we may, like him, relinquish duality and experience the two worlds as one.

Beware! You are half-musk and half-dung. Beware! Do not
build up the dung, build up the Chinese musk!

(M V: 2479)

Don't put musk on your body, rub it on your heart!
What is musk? The holy name of God.
The hypocrite puts musk on his body
and puts his spirit on the dung heap.

(M II: 266–7)

In earlier chapters, we saw this opposition at work in the characters of
Abraham and Nimrod, Moses and Pharaoh, Jesus and his ass, and with
the falcon and the owl, and the hoopoe and the crow. In these
relationships, the opposites are to a greater or lesser extent in conflict
with each other, and thus illustrate the tug-of-war between our higher
and lower selves. Rumi also provides us with examples of a very different
kind of relationship, one that is based on a common purpose rather than
opposition: Layla and Majnun, Mahmud and Ayaz, the nightingale and
the rose, the king and the falcon. The relationships based on opposition
are mirrors for ourselves in our state of separation; those based on a
common purpose reflect the relationship between the lover and the
Beloved, either in the heart's yearning to be reunited with its beloved,
or in its total surrender to its lord. The union of lover and Beloved is the
subject of the following passages from the *Mathnawi* and *Fihi mafihi*.

THE ONE WITH NO OPPOSITE

A certain person knocked at a friend's door. The
friend asked, 'Who is there?'
He answered, 'I.' The friend said, 'Go away! The time
is not right. There is no place here for those who are
raw.'
How will those who are raw be cooked, but in the fire
of absence and separation? What else will free them from
hypocrisy?

The poor fellow went away and wandered for a whole year, consumed by the fire of separation.

When he was cooked, he returned and paced up and down in front of his friend's house.

His knock at the friend's door was both fearful and respectful, for he was afraid of saying anything discourteous.

The friend called out, 'Who is there?' He replied, ''Tis thou, oh charmer of hearts.'

'Now,' said the friend, 'since thou am I, come in O Self, for there is no room in this house for two 'I's'.

The double end of the thread will not pass through the eye of the needle; but since you are single, come into the needle.'

How can the body of the camel be thinned to a single thread, except with the shears of spiritual practices and actions?

And that requires the Hand of God, for it is the *Be, and it was* of all seemingly impossible things.

By His Hand, every impossible thing is made possible . . .

The thread is now single. Do not be led astray when you see *B* and *E* as two letters.

B and *E* are pulled tight like a noose, drawing the Unmanifest into manifestation.

The noose is double in the world of manifest forms, yet those two letters are single in Reality.

(M I: 3056–69, 3078–80)

With God, there is no room for two 'I's'. You say 'I' and He says 'I'. Either you must die before Him or He die before you, for duality to disappear. However, it is impossible for Him to die, both phenomenally or conceptually, since He is *the Living One, the Undying* [Q 25:58]. He is so gracious that, were it possible, He would die for you so that duality might vanish. Now since it is impossible for Him to die, you must die so that He may manifest Himself to you and duality may disappear.

(F 6: A36/T26)

Because my genus is not that of my Lord, my ego passed
away for the sake of His ego.
With the passing away of my ego, He remained alone. I
whirl like dust under the feet of His horse.
The individual self turned to dust, in which only His
footprints remain.
Become dust under His feet for the sake of His
footprints, so that you may become His crown.

(M II: 1173–6)

Rumi on philosophers and scholars

One of the reasons often given for Baha'uddin Walad's departure from
Khorasan is his conflict with the philosopher Razi. Although the
hostility of philosophers towards the Sufis was nothing new, it is
exemplified in an anecdote related by Wassaf in his 'History', the
Tarikh-i Wassaf. According to Wassaf, in the time of Baha'uddin Walad,
the Khwarizmshah was favourably inclined towards the Sufis. This
annoyed Razi, who ordered two workers from the king's stable to be
dressed in Sufi robes and then surrounded by a number of people
pretending to be their pupils and followers. The king was asked to
meet them, and in their presence he assumed the role of a humble
devotee, earnestly requesting their advice. Razi later revealed the true
identity of the so-called 'Sufis', pointing out to the king that the
deceptive nature of appearances meant that even stable-hands could
pose as enlightened spiritual guides (Iqbal, *The Life and Work of
Rumi*, p. 54).

Rumi's own attitude to philosophers and scholars, which may
have been influenced by his father, Baha'uddin Walad, and Imam
Ghazali, is illustrated by Aflaki's account of the learned professor who
took his students to pay their respects to Rumi. Along the way, the
young men agreed to put some questions to Rumi on points
of Arabic grammar, with the intention of comparing his knowledge
with that of their illustrious professor, whom they looked upon as
unequalled.

When the visitors were seated before him, Rumi addressed them on various relevant subjects for a while and then told them the following anecdote.

'A simple jurist and an Arabic grammarian were travelling together when they chanced upon a dilapidated well. The sight inspired the jurist to recite the Qur'anic text, *"How many sinful people have We destroyed? How many cities now lie in ruins, their lofty palaces uninhabited and their wells abandoned? [Q 22:45]"* He pronounced the Arabic word *bir* (well), with the vowel prolonged. The grammarian instantly objected, telling the jurist that in order to fulfil the requirements of classical purity he should pronounce the word with a short vowel and hiatus, as *bi'r*.

'The two men now engaged in fierce argument over the correct pronunciation. The dispute lasted the rest of the day and well into the night. They combed through the pages of book after book to bolster their own theory about the word's pronunciation. Unable to settle their dispute, each contender remained firmly entrenched in his own opinion.

'Now it so happened that in the dark the grammarian lost his footing and fell into the well, from the bottom of which he appealed to the jurist for help, "O my most courteous fellow-traveller, help me get out of this loathsome pit."

'The jurist at once said he would be only too happy to help him, but he attached a minor condition: the grammarian had to admit that he was wrong and agree to omit the hiatus in the word *bi'r*. The grammarian's answer was "Never", and so in the well he remained.'

'Now, as for yourselves,' said Rumi, 'until you are willing to rid your hearts of the "hiatus" of indecision and self-love, you can never hope to get out of the loathsome pit of self-worship – the source of human greed and lust. Joseph was imprisoned in a well. Your prison is the well of "self-worship" in your hearts; and you will not escape from it, nor will you attain to those heavenly regions – *the spacious refuge of Allah* [Q 4:99]. *For Allah's earth is vast, those who persevere shall receive reward without measure. Lo I am commanded to serve Allah and worship none but Him* [Q 39:10–11].'

On hearing these words, the entire gathering of students bowed their heads before Rumi and declared themselves to be his followers.

(Aflaki, *Legends of the Sufis*, pp. 31–2)

Rumi addresses the same theme in the following passage from *Fihi mafihi*.

The great scholars of the age split hairs over all manner of sciences. They have a complete knowledge and understanding of things that do not concern them directly. But as for what is truly important and of greater concern to him than anything else, namely his own self, your great scholar has no knowledge. He pronounces on the legality or illegality of everything, saying, 'This is permitted, and that is not,' or, 'This is lawful, and that is unlawful.' Yet he does not know his own self, whether it is lawful or unlawful, pure or impure.'

(F 4: A30/T19)

Rumi makes a similar point in a brief anecdote in the *Mathnawi*.

A man with a greying beard rushed into a barber's, saying, 'Quick! I'm getting married. Take all the grey hairs out of my beard.'

The barber cut off the whole of the man's beard, and gave it to him, saying, 'There! *You* pick them out if you want to. I have more important matters to attend to.'

That 'pick them out' is the method of theologians; the true spiritual seeker is not interested in splitting hairs.

(M III: 1376–9)

Two more anecdotes – one from *Fihi mafihi*, the other from the *Mathnawi* – are included here to show how each time Rumi appears to return to a particular theme, he is actually presenting it in a slightly different way in order to drive his point home.

> A Sufi was seated before a grammarian. The grammarian said, 'All words fall into one of three categories: verbs, nouns or particles.'
>
> The Sufi rent his robe, and lamented aloud, 'Woe is me! Twenty years of my life, twenty years of striving and seeking, have all been in vain. I laboured all these years in the hope that there was another word beyond these, and now you have destroyed my hopes!'
>
> The Sufi had in fact found the word he was looking for, and had thus attained his goal, but he said this in order to awaken the grammarian.
>
> (F 42: A165/T164)

> A certain self-conceited grammarian boarded a boat. Turning to the boatman, he asked, 'Have you ever studied grammar?'
>
> 'No,' replied the boatman.
>
> 'Well, then,' said the grammarian, 'Half your life has been wasted.'
>
> Disheartened, the boatman refrained from answering. Later, when the boat was caught in a whirlpool, the boatman called out to the grammarian, 'Tell me, can you swim?'
>
> 'No, my good man,' replied the grammarian.
>
> 'Oh, grammarian,' said the boatman. 'Your whole life has been wasted, because the boat is sinking into this whirlpool.'
>
> Know that here self-effacement (*mahw*) is what is required, not grammar (*nahw*). If you are dead to the self (*mahw*), you can plunge into the ocean without fear. The water of the ocean buoys up one who is dead, but how can

those who are living escape from the ocean? When you have died to your lower nature, the Ocean of Divine Consciousness will raise you on high.

(M I: 2835–43)

The following passage from the *Mathnawi*, which echoes Rumi's earlier definition of the two kinds of intelligence, illustrates the difference between the knowledge of the Sufis (the men of heart) and that of philosophers and other 'thinkers' (the men of body).

> The knowledge of the men of heart lifts them up; the knowledge of the men of body weighs them down.
>
> When knowledge comes from the heart, it is a friend; when knowledge comes from the body, it is a burden.
>
> God said, *Like an ass laden with books* [Q 62:5]; knowledge that comes not from Him is burdensome.
>
> Knowledge that does not come directly from God is like the rouged cheeks of a crone.
>
> Nevertheless, if you bear this burden in the right spirit, it will be removed and you will obtain spiritual joy.
>
> So long as you do not carry this burden out of pride or selfish desire, you will discover the source of knowledge within you.
>
> When you mount upon the steed of true knowledge, the burden will fall from your shoulders.
>
> Unless you drink His wine, how will you be free from selfish desires, O you who seek no more of Him than His name?
>
> What does His name suggest? The idea of Him. And the idea of Him guides you to union with Him.
>
> Do you know a name that doesn't refer to the thing named? Have you ever plucked a rose from the letters R,O,S,E?
>
> You say His name, now seek the reality behind the name! Look for the moon in the sky, not in its reflection in a lake.

If you want to go beyond names and letters, erase the self with one stroke.

Be like a polished sword, free from tarnish. Work to become a polished mirror, free of rust.

Cleanse yourself of all the attributes of self, so that you may see your own pure and untarnished essence!

Behold in your own heart all the knowledge of the prophets, without books, without learning, without teacher.

(M I: 3445–61)

PREDESTINATION AND FREE WILL

These subjects, which are much debated by philosophers and theologians, are addressed by Rumi in the story about a man who flees from Azrael (the Angel of Death) and ends up in the place appointed for his demise.

One morning a man came rushing into Solomon's hall of justice, his face as white as a sheet. 'What on earth is the matter?' asked Solomon.

'It was Azrael,' replied the man. 'He gave me such a look, filled with anger and contempt.'

'Come now,' said Solomon. 'Ask of me any favour you like.'

'O protector of lives,' said the man. 'Command the wind to take me to Hindustan. Once there my life should be safe.'

How people flee from spiritual poverty into the jaws of greed and vain hope! Fear of poverty is like the terror of the man in this story, greed and hope the Hindustan.

Solomon commanded the wind to carry the man swiftly across the ocean to Hindustan. The next morning, when Solomon was holding audience, he asked Azrael, 'Why did you give that Muslim such an angry look that you drove him from his home?'

'I didn't look at him in anger,' replied the Angel of

Death. 'I was just surprised to see him, since God had
instructed me to take his spirit in Hindustan yesterday. So I
looked at him in amazement, thinking to myself that, even
if he had a hundred wings, he would never get to our
rendezvous in Hindustan in time.'

Judge all affairs of this world by the same rule. Open your
eyes so that you may see! Who are we running away from?
From ourselves? How absurd! From God? How criminal!

(M I: 956–70)

Rumi's understanding of the paradox whereby an action is
simultaneously an act of God – or God's decree (*qaza*) – and an act of
free will (*ikhtiyar*) is explained by Franklin D. Lewis:

> Rumi holds that only saintly ones with spiritual insight can
> comprehend this mystery of free will and divine decree
> (MI:1466). If our spiritual eyes and ears are pure enough,
> we perceive God's inspiration (*vahy*) and choose the right
> course, which is also the course that God has destined for
> us. Both predestination and free will exist simultaneously,
> and as a proverbial saying undoubtedly known to Rumi
> phrased it, 'Belief lies between predestination and free will.'
>
> (Lewis, *Rumi*, pp. 413–14)

The paradox is expressed succinctly in the following verses from the
Mathnawi. The second passage, in which 'thought' is also counted as
'action', concerns a dervish, who, having failed to find a hidden
treasure, turns to God for help.

> Read the interpretations of the verse from the Qur'an: *It*
>   *was not you who slayed them, but God who slayed them*
>   [Q 8:17].
> If we fire an arrow, it is not we who fire it. We are the
>   bow; the arrow is fired by God.
>
> (M I: 615–6)

In answer to his prayers, he heard a Voice from heaven,
    saying,
'You were told to put the arrow to the bow, but when
    were you told to fire it with all your strength?
Pride of self caused you to raise the bow high and use all
    your skill as an archer.
Renounce this skill. Put the arrow to the bow, but do not
    draw the bowstring tight.
Where the arrow falls, dig and search. Don't trust in your
    own strength; seek the treasure with humility.'
What you are looking for is *nearer to you than your jugular*
    vein [Q 50:16]; you fired the arrow of thought too far.

(M VI: 2347–53)

Our thought is an arrow shot by Him. Does the
arrow stay in the air? No, it returns to Him.

(M I: 1143)

Free will is the endeavour to thank God for his
beneficence. Predestination is the denial of that
beneficence.
    Gratefulness for the power of free will, increases that
power; predestination takes the Divine gift of free
will away from you.

(M I: 938–9)

LOVE

Love is the glue that holds the Divine Unity together, and our
transition from duality to nonduality, from existence to non-existence,
is effected through the activity of Divine Love, of which human love is
but a pale reflection. This transition can be a painful process, however,
for we tend to experience the effects of Love as suffering. And yet the
suffering we experience can perhaps be described as our resistance to
the Divine Call to abandon the self and become re-absorbed in the
Unity of Being. As Afzal Iqbal says, 'Love solves all the mysteries of the

world; it is at once an ailment and a matchless cure' (Iqbal, *The Life and Work of Jalaluddin Rumi*, p. 242). In Rumi's words:

> Through love bitter things become sweet,
> Through love bits of copper are turned to gold.
> Through love dregs become purest wine;
> Through love pain becomes a healing balm.
> Through love the dead become alive . . .

> (M II: 1529–31)

Elsewhere, Rumi likens love to an astrolabe (a navigational aid), when he says:

> The lover's ailment is unlike any other ailment:
> Love is the astrolabe of the mysteries of God.
> Whether love is from earth or from heaven,
> It leads us to God.

> (M I: 110–11)

But he adds immediately:

> However much I might try to expound or explain Love,
> When I come to Love itself I am ashamed of my
>   explanations . . .
> In trying to explain Love, the intellect fell down in the mud
>   like an ass.
> Love alone can explain the mysteries of love and lovers.

> (M I: 112, 115)

Finally, here are two further examples of Rumi's writing on the theme of love. The first is the Song of the Reed, which forms the opening verses of the *Mathnawi*, the second is from the *Divan*.

> Listen to the reed and the tale it tells
>   as it laments of separation:

'Ever since I was cut from the reed-bed
　　my refrain has moved men and women to tears.
I want a heart torn open by separation
　　to share the pain of love's yearning.
Every one who has been parted from his source
　　longs for the day he returns to that state of union.
At gatherings the haunting tune I play is heard
　　alike by the sad at heart and the joyful.
Every one hears my song according to his emotional state;
　　yet not one of them searches out the secrets that lie within.
My secrets are not different from the plaint of my lament,
　　but they can not be perceived by the physical senses.
The body is not veiled from the soul, nor the soul from the body,
　　yet no one has ever seen the soul.'
The sound of the reed is made from fire, not breath;
　　and whoever does not have this fire might as well be dead!
It is Love's fire that ignites the reed,
　　It is Love's ferment that permeates the wine.
The reed is the companion of broken-hearted lovers;
　　its refrain reveals our innermost secrets.
Have you ever seen a poison and an antidote like the reed?
　　Have you ever seen a more sympathetic lover?
The reed describes the bloodstained Path of Love,
　　and tells stories about the passion of Majnun.
But just as the tongue speaks only to the ear,
　　so this particular sense is only for the sense-less.
In our grief the days have become protracted,
　　days wherein pain and sorrow go hand-in-hand.
If our time is spent, let it go – it doesn't matter.
　　That which remains is Thou, as Thou art!
Anyone but a fish soon has their fill of water;
　　anyone who has no daily bread finds the day long.
No one who is 'raw' understands what it is to be 'ripe',
　　and so my discourse must be brief.

(M I: 1–18)

A soul not clothed with Love
brings shame on its existence.
Be drunk on Love,
for Love is all that exists.
They ask, 'What is Love?'
Say, 'Renouncing your will.'
He who has not renounced will
has no will at all.
The lover is a mighty king,
standing above the two worlds.
A king does not look
at what is beneath him.
Only Love and lovers
have eternal life.
Set your heart on this alone;
the rest is merely borrowed . . .

(D 455: A1:54)

Chapter Eight

Discourses from
Fihi mafihi

EXTRACT FROM THE FIRST DISCOURSE

Rumi's commentary on a verse from the Qur'an

To emphasize a point he is making in the opening discourse of *Fihi mafihi*, Rumi quotes the Arab proverb 'We have learned in order to give, not in order to take'. The proverb prompts him to interrupt the flow of his talk to deliver a lengthy commentary on a verse from the Qur'an. The commentary is included here as an example of Rumi's exposition of the Qur'an and the Prophetic Traditions (the Sunnah of the Prophet Muhammad), but it also gives an insight into the Prophet's perception of his mission to the tribes of pagan Arabs. The Qur'anic verse itself refers to events following the Prophet Muhammad's victory at the battle of Badr in AD 624, one of the battles fought by the armies of Medina in the Holy War (*jihad*) against the forces of Mecca. As Rumi makes clear, however, the real battle – the Greater Holy War – is the eternal conflict between our human will and the Divine Will. The teaching contained in the commentary therefore has a timeless relevance, a factor that becomes apparent when, towards the end of his discourse, Rumi applies it to the predicament in which Islam then found itself due to the actions of the Parvana of Rum, the powerful Seljuk vizier and admirer of Rumi.

At this point I am minded to comment on a verse from the Qur'an, even though it is not relevant to the present discourse. However, since the thought occurs to me now, I may as well expound it. God says: *O Prophet, say to those captives who are in your hands, 'If God knows there to be any good in your hearts He will give you better than that which has been taken from you, and He will forgive you, for God is All-forgiving, All-Merciful* [Q 8:70]. This verse was revealed in the following circumstances. The blessed Prophet had defeated the unbelievers, with much slaughter and plundering. He also took many prisoners and had them shackled hand and foot. Among those captured was the Prophet's uncle, Abbas. The prisoners wailed all night long in their chains, bemoaning their misery and humiliation. Having abandoned all hope, they were expecting to be put to the sword. When the Prophet saw them, he laughed.

'You see,' exclaimed the prisoners, 'he is human after all. The claim that he is not human is false. He looks at us, sees prisoners in their shackles, and rejoices. That is how it is with men who are governed by their passions – when they triumph over their enemies and see them beaten, they are jubilant.'

'Not so,' said the Prophet, reading what was in their minds. 'I am not laughing because I see my enemies defeated, nor because I see your affliction. I am laughing because with my inner eye I see myself dragging a group of people in chains out of Hell's fiery furnace by force and drawing them into heavenly Paradise and the eternal rose garden. Yet they are wailing and lamenting, saying, "Why are you taking us from this place of perdition into that haven and rose-bower?" That is why I am laughing. Since you have not yet been given the vision to understand clearly what I am saying, God commands me: "Say to the prisoners: 'First you gathered together your armies, and mustered much strength, trusting completely in your own might, virtue, and force of arms. You said to yourselves that we will do this and that, and we will defeat the Muslims and utterly vanquish them. You did not imagine there could be One mightier than yourselves. You did not know of One more powerful than you. Now that all your plans have turned out contrary to your designs, you are trembling with fear. Even so, you have not repented of your affliction. You are in despair, yet you still cannot see there is One mightier than you. It is therefore necessary for Me to show you My might and power, and for you to see yourselves subject to My will so that things may be made easy for you. Do not despair of Me in your present fear, for I am able to deliver you from this fear and lead you to safety. He who is able to bring forth a white cow from a black one is also able to bring forth a black cow from a white one. *He causes the night to pass into the day, and He causes the day to pass into the night* [Q 35:13]. *He brings forth the living from the dead, and he brings forth the dead out of the living* [Q 30:19]. Now, in your present state as prisoners, do not abandon hope of My presence in order that I may take you by the hand, for *no one despairs of God's mercy, except the people who have no faith* [Q 12:87]"'.'

The Prophet continued, saying, 'God says, "O prisoners, if you turn from your former belief and perceive Me in My states of fear and hope, and perceive that you are subject to My will in all circumstances, I will release you from your present fear. I will also restore to you all the property that has been plundered from you and which you have lost. Indeed, I will restore to you many times as much, and more. I will pardon you, and to your prosperity in this world I will join prosperity in the next".'

'I repent,' said Abbas. 'I have turned my back on my former ways.'

The Prophet said, 'God requires a token of this claim you are now making.'

It is easy to boast of love,
But the proof of it is otherwise.

'In God's name, what token do you require?' asked Abbas.

'Give all your remaining wealth to the army of Islam, so that the army of Islam may be strengthened,' replied the Prophet. 'That is, if you have truly become a Muslim and desire the good of Islam and the community of Islam.'

'O Apostle of God, what do I have left,' said Abbas. 'Everything has been plundered. I do not even have an old straw mat to my name.'

'You see,' said the Prophet, 'you have not become righteous. You have not yet abandoned your old ways. I will tell you how much property you have, where you have hidden it, to whom you have entrusted it, and where it is buried.'

'Oh, no!' exclaimed Abbas.

'Did you not entrust a portion to your mother? Did you not bury it under a certain wall? Did you not specify that if you returned safely she was to give it to you, and if you did not return she was to spend it on this or that object, give so much to so-and-so, and keep so much for herself?'

On hearing these words, Abbas raised his finger as a token of his acceptance of the faith.

'O Prophet,' he said, 'in all honesty I used to think the heavens held you in special favour, like the kings of long ago, Haman, Shaddad, and Nimrod. When you uttered those words, I knew for certain that this special favour is divine in origin.'

'Now you are speaking the truth,' said the Prophet. 'This time I heard your inner girdle of doubt break. The sound of it snapping reached the ear hidden within the inner depths of my soul. Whenever anyone's girdle of doubt, polytheism, or unbelief snaps, I can hear it with my inner ear, the ear of my soul. Now you have truly become a righteous man and professed the faith.'

(F I: A14–17/T4–5)

Rumi then proceeds to give the following explanation for his commentary:

All of this I related to the Parvana. I told him, 'You presented yourself as the leader of the Islamic community, saying, "I am making a sacrifice of myself, my intellect, my powers of deliberation and judgement, so that Islam may continue to prosper and spread." But since you relied on your own judgement and did not look to God in the knowledge that everything proceeds from Him, God turned your endeavours into a means for bringing about the diminution of Islam. Having united forces with the Tartars, you are helping them to destroy the Syrians and Egyptians and thus devastate the realm of Islam. The very endeavour that was intended to secure the survival of Islam has become the means of its diminution.'

(F I: A17/T5–6)

Having reprimanded the Parvana thus, Rumi tells him what he needs to do in order to bring about a possible reversal of the situation. He continues:

God works in mysterious ways. Things may look good on the outside, but there may be evil lurking within them. For this reason no one should allow his pride to delude him into thinking that he is himself the originator of a good idea or a good action. If things were really as they appear to be, the Prophet, with his enlightened vision and insight, would not have cried out, 'Lord, show me things as they are! You make a thing appear beautiful when in reality it is ugly. You make a thing appear ugly when in reality it is beautiful. Therefore show us each thing as it is, lest we become ensnared and constantly led astray.' Now your judgement, however good and enlightened it may be, is clearly not better than that of the Prophet, and yet he spoke as he did. So don't now rely on your every thought and inclination. Humble yourself before God, and be ever fearful of Him.

(F I: A18/T6–7)

EXTRACT FROM THE FOURTH DISCOURSE

'We come into this world for a specific purpose . . .'

The discourse opens with an unnamed person casually remarking, 'I
have forgotten to do something.' From this simple beginning, Rumi
builds a discourse to remind us that there is one thing which must
never be forgotten: we came into this world for a specific purpose, for
a particular function that can only be performed by human beings. We
were created to be God's vicegerent, and our special function in
creation is the 'Trust' referred to in the verse from the Qur'an (33:72)
quoted by Rumi in the opening paragraph of the discourse. If we fulfil
this purpose, we eradicate wrongdoing and folly from our lives; if we
do not, we will have done nothing with our lives.

> There is one thing in this world that should never be
> forgotten. You may forget everything else, but as long as
> you do not forget this one thing there is no cause for
> concern. If you remember everything else but forget this
> one thing, you will have achieved nothing at all. It is as
> though a king had sent you into the country with a specific
> mission. You go, and perform a hundred other tasks. But if
> you neglect to perform the particular task for which you
> were sent into the country, it will be as though you had
> done nothing. Human beings come into this world for a
> specific purpose. If they do not fulfil this purpose, they
> achieve nothing. We *offered the Trust unto the heavens and
> the earth and the mountains, and they refused to undertake it,
> being afraid thereof; but man undertook it. Truly, he has
> wronged himself and been foolish* [Q 33:72].
>   'We offered the faith to the heavens, but they were
> unable to accept it.' Consider how many feats the heavens
> perform that bewilder human reason: they turn rocks into
> rubies and carnelians; they turn mountains into gold and
> silver mines; they give life to the plants, causing them to
> spring forth and create a veritable Garden of Eden. The
> earth also receives seed and brings forth fruit; it covers up

blemishes; it performs innumerable miraculous feats. The mountains also give forth diverse minerals. All these things they do, yet that one thing they cannot do: that one thing is for humankind to do. *And We have honoured the children of Adam* [Q 17:70]. God did not say, 'We have honoured the heavens and the earth.' So it is for humankind to do what the heavens and the earth and the mountains cannot do. When it performs that task, there is no more wrongdoing and folly.

You may object, saying, 'Even though I have not accomplished that one task, I have done a lot of other things.' But you did not come into the world to do these other things. It is like taking a priceless sword made from Indian steel, of the kind found in royal treasure houses, and using it as a cleaver to cut up offal, saying, 'I am not letting this sword stand idle, I am putting it to good use.' Or it is like taking a bowl made of solid gold and using it to cook turnips, when an ounce of the same gold could buy a hundred cooking pots. Or it is like taking an exquisitely crafted dagger of the finest tempered steel and using it as a nail on which to hang a broken gourd, saying, 'I am making excellent use of this dagger. By hanging a gourd from it I am not letting it stand idle.' What a ludicrous state of affairs! When the gourd could be hung from a nail that costs next to nothing, where is the sense in hanging it from a dagger worth a hundred dinars? God has set a high price on you, as He says, *God has purchased from the faithful their souls and their possessions in return for the Garden [of Paradise]* [Q 9:111].

You are worth more than both heaven and earth.
What can I do if you do not know not your own worth?
    [Sana'i, *Hadiqat al-haqiqa*.]

Do not undersell yourself, for in God's eyes you are
    worth much. [Rumi, *Divan-i Shams-i Tabrizi*.]

God says, 'I have bought you, your breath, your possessions, and your lives. If they are spent on Me, and given to Me, their price is eternal Paradise. This is what you are worth to Me.' But if you sell yourself to hell, it is yourself you will have wronged, just like the man who nails a dagger worth a hundred dinars into the wall and hangs a pot or gourd on it.

You make excuses for yourself, saying that you are engaged in all sorts of high-minded projects. You say you are studying jurisprudence, philosophy, logic, astronomy, medicine, and so on. Who are you doing all these things for if not for yourself? You study jurisprudence so that no one can steal your bread, strip you of your clothes, or kill you. This is all for your own peace of mind. In the case of astronomy, your study of the movements of the planets and their influence on the earth, and whether this is beneficial or detrimental, is all related to your own situation. This is all for yourself. Astrological portents are related to your own ascendant. This again serves your own ends. If you consider the question carefully, you will see that you are the root of the matter. These other things are merely branches of yourself.

If these things that are branches of yourself, encompass so many wondrous phases and worlds within worlds, consider what you who are their root must be like! If your branches have their apogees and nadirs, their lucky and unlucky aspects, consider what apogees and nadirs you must have on the spiritual plane. What lucky and unlucky portents, what benefits and impairments! Such a spirit possesses this property, is able to produce this, and is suited for such a task.

Your life is sustained by more than just eating and sleeping. You have another food. As the Prophet said, 'I pass the night in the presence of my Lord, and He gives me food and drink.' In this lower world you have forgotten that heavenly food and busy yourself with the food of this world. Day and night you nurture your body. Now this body is your horse, and this world is its stable. The horse's food is not food for its rider. The rider has his own kind of sustenance. But because you are ruled by your bestial and animal nature, you have remained in the stable with the horses instead of taking your place in the ranks of the kings and princes of the spiritual world. Your heart dwells there, but because you are ruled by your body you obey its orders, and so you remain imprisoned by your body.

Such was the case with Majnun, when he was headed toward Layla's dwelling-place. So long as he was fully conscious, he drove his camel in that direction. But whenever his mind wandered and filled itself with thoughts of Layla, he forgot about his camel. The camel took advantage of this lapse in concentration to head back to a certain village where it had its offspring. When he came to his senses Majnun found that he had journeyed for two days in the wrong direction. Things went on like this for three months, until he eventually cried out, 'This camel is my undoing!' At which he jumped down from the camel and continued on foot, singing to himself:

'My camel's desire is behind me; my own desire lies ahead:
Truly, she and I are at odds and can agree no more.'

(F 4: A26–9/T15–18)

EXTRACTS FROM THE SIXTH DISCOURSE

Anecdote about the king and the poet

These words are for the person who needs words in order to understand. But a person who can understand without the medium of words, why would he need words? Heaven and earth are all words for a person with understanding, for he is born of the words *'Be!' and it is* [Q 36:82]. What need of shouting and screaming has the person who can hear a whisper?

An Arabic-speaking poet once appeared before a

king. The king, who was a Turk, did not even know Persian. The poet had composed an elaborate poem in Arabic to honour the king. When the king was seated on his throne and all of his courtiers and ministers were in their appropriate places, the poet rose and began to recite his poem. Whenever verses meriting approval were read, the king nodded his head; at verses that provoked astonishment, he looked amazed, and at verses that expressed humility, he listened attentively.

His bewildered courtiers murmured amongst themselves, saying, 'Our king did not know a single word of Arabic. How can it be that he nodded his head in all the right places? Could it be that he has known Arabic all these years but kept it concealed from us? Woe betide us if we have ever said anything discourteous in Arabic!'

The courtiers approach the king's favourite slave, giving him a horse, a camel, and a sum of money. They promised him as much again, saying, 'Find out for us whether or not the king knows Arabic. If he doesn't, how was it that he nodded his head in all the right places? Was it a miracle or divine inspiration?'

One day the slave found the right moment while the king was out hunting. The king was in a good mood because much game had been taken, and so, when the slave asked him, he burst out laughing. 'By God, I don't know Arabic,' he replied. 'As for nodding my head and showing approval, I knew what his purpose had been when he composed the poem and so I nodded and showed approval. It was self-evident that the root of the matter was the purpose. The poem was merely a branch of this. Had there been no purpose, he would not have composed the poem.'

If you look to the purpose, there is no duality. Duality is present in the branches; the root is one. This is how it is with Sufi shaykhs. Outwardly they differ in their states, acts, and words, but in their purpose they are one thing only, and that is the quest for God.

(F 6: A33–4/T23–4)

The fault you see in another lies within yourself

The Sufis' profound understanding of human psychology is illustrated in the following extract from the Sixth Discourse which, although written over 700 years ago, offers a succinct analysis of the modern psychological phenomenon known as 'projection':

> If you perceive a fault in your brother, the fault that you see in him lies within yourself. The things of this world are like a mirror in which you see your own image, for 'The believer is the mirror for his fellow believer.' Get rid of the fault in yourself, because what distresses you in others lies within you.
>
> An elephant was led to a well to drink. When it saw itself in the water, it shied away. It thought it was shying away from another elephant, not realizing that it was shying away from itself.
>
> You are not offended by negative qualities such as injustice, hatred, envy, greed, harshness, or pride when they are within yourself. But when you see them in another, you feel offended and shy away. A person does not find his own scab or abscess repellent; he will dip his infected hand into the stew and lick his fingers without feeling the least bit squeamish. But if he sees a tiny cut or abscess on another's hand, he has no stomach for the stew that man's hand has been dipped in. Negative qualities are just like scabs and abscesses; you are not offended by them when they are within yourself, but when you see the least hint of them in another you take great offence. Just as you shy away from another, so you should excuse them when they shy away from you, offended. The pain you feel is his excuse for shying away, because your pain comes from seeing the same faults he sees. The Prophet said, 'The believer is the mirror for his fellow believer.' He did not say, 'The unbeliever is the mirror of the unbeliever.' This was not because the unbeliever is not a mirror for others, but because he is unaware of the mirror of his own heart.

(F 6: A35–6/T25)

EXTRACTS FROM THE TWENTY-SIXTH DISCOURSE

The teacher and the fur coat

Rumi tells us that in the time of the Prophet Muhammad a certain person said to the Prophet, 'I don't want this religion [*islam*]. By God, I don't want it! Take it back! Ever since I entered this religion of yours I have not had a single day of peace. I have lost my wealth, my wife, and my children. My honour, strength, and passion have all gone.' The Prophet replied, 'Wherever our religion goes, it does not come back until it has uprooted a person and swept his house clean' (F 26; A125/T120). Rumi explains the significance of the Prophet's words, and then returns to the person's complaint about the suffering caused by his *islam*.

> Since nothing in either this world or the next is achieved without suffering, dedicate your suffering with the next world in mind so that your suffering does not go to waste.
>
> You say, 'O Muhammad, take this religion away from me, for it gives me no peace.' Yet how can religion let go of a person before it brings him to the goal?
>
> There is a story about a certain teacher who was so poor that when winter came he had nothing to wear but a thin cotton garment. One day, as chance would have it, a flood swept a bear down from the mountain. Some children caught sight of it, but as the bear's head was under water they could only see its back. 'Teacher!' they shouted. 'Look! There's a fur coat in the water. Since you're suffering from the cold, grab hold of it.'
>
> Driven by a combination of cold and need, the teacher jumped into the water to fish out the fur coat. No sooner had he done this than the bear dug its claws into him and held on tight.
>
> The children called out, 'Teacher, either bring out the fur coat or, if you can't, let go of it and you come out!'
>
> 'I've let go of the fur coat,' answered the teacher, 'but it won't let go of me! What am I to do?'

How can your yearning for God let go of you? . . .
Fishermen do not reel a fish in in one go. When the hook
catches in the fish's mouth, they reel it in a little so that its
strength bleeds out of it. They keep letting it out and
reeling it in until all the fight in it has gone. When God
catches a person with the hook of Love, he reels him in
gradually so that, little by little, the fight is drained out of
him. *God straitens and bestows* [Q 2:245].

(F 26: A126–7/T121, 122)

Learning the first lesson

If these words seem repetitious to you, it is because you
have not yet learned the first lesson, and so it is necessary
to repeat the same thing over again every day.

There was once a teacher who had taught a child for
three months, but his pupil did not progress beyond 'A has
nothing'. The child's father came to the teacher and said, 'I
have not failed to pay your fees. If I have failed, tell me and
I will give you more.'

'The failure is not yours,' replied the teacher. 'It's just
that the child is not making any progress.'

The teacher called the child and said, 'Say "A has
nothing".'

'Has nothing,' said the child, who was unable to say
'A'.

'Now you see what the problem is,' said the teacher.
'Since he hasn't progressed beyond this point, and hasn't
even learned this, how can we go on to the next lesson?'

(F 26: A128/T123)

DISCOURSE TWENTY-SEVEN

Food unfit for a dervish

Rumi's frequent references to fasting apply to more than just physical
food. By fasting, he means abstaining from the things of this world that

satisfy the hunger of our lower nature. Such things are fodder for the ass. In this brief discourse, he offers us another analogy in which he equates the 'food' of this world with the food offered by a beautiful young girl, who is herself a metaphor for the 'world of attraction' or 'world of appearances'. The effect her food has on the dervish in the story illustrates the extent to which we need to be aware of the 'food' we eat.

> It is better not to ask questions of a dervish, for to do so is to oblige him to invent a lie. Why? When a materialistic person asks him a question, he has to reply. He cannot answer him with the truth, since the questioner is not worthy of such an answer, nor is he able to receive it. His mouth and lips are not worthy of such a morsel. So the dervish has to answer him according to the questioner's capacity, by inventing a lie in order to be rid of him. Even though everything a dervish says is truth and not a lie, when compared with what the true answer is for the dervish, the answer he gives the questioner is a lie; yet for the person who hears it, it is right, and even more than right.
>
> A dervish once had a disciple who used to beg for him. One day, from the proceeds of his begging, he took a morsel to his master. The dervish ate the morsel, and that night experienced a nocturnal emission.
>
> 'From whom did you get that food?' he asked the disciple.
>
> 'It was given to me by a beautiful girl,' replied the disciple.
>
> 'By God!' said the dervish. 'It's twenty years since I had a nocturnal emission. This is the effect her morsel had on me.'
>
> Dervishes must therefore be mindful and not eat the food of just anyone, because dervishes are subtly refined and easily affected by things. Things have an effect on them, showing up in the way a speck of grime shows up on a clean white robe. With a dirty robe, one that has become soiled from years of being exposed to grime and dirt and

lost all its whiteness, regardless of how much dirt and grease are rubbed into it, nothing will show. This being the case, dervishes should not eat any morsel from wrongdoers, those who live basely, or materialists. Morsels from such strangers have an effect on the dervish, influencing his thoughts and corrupting them, just as the dervish experienced nocturnal emission from eating the morsel of that girl.

(F 27: A131–2/T126–7)

EXTRACT FROM THE FIFTIETH DISCOURSE

The countryman who ate halva for the first time

In his writings, Rumi often quotes the proverbial saying, 'Things are made clear by their opposites'. In the following anecdote he applies this saying to the contrast between the food of this world and *real* food. Unlike the former, the latter is sweetness itself: once we have tasted it, we have no choice but to follow our heart.

A countryman once stayed with a friend who lived in the town. His host gave his guest some *halva*, which he tucked into with great gusto. Turning to his host, he said, 'I've spent my entire life eating nothing but carrots. Now that I've tasted *halva*, carrots don't appeal to me any more. Now, I won't be able to have *halva* whenever I want, and yet I no longer want what I had before. What am I to do?' When the countryman tasted halva, he was drawn to live in the town. The townsman had captured his heart, and so he had no choice but to follow his heart.

(F 50: A196–7/T197)

Chapter Nine

Tales from the *Mathnawi*

Rumi's response to a critic

The fact that the *Mathnawi* appears to follow no clearly defined systematic development can be disconcerting. So can its admixture of anecdotal stories and commentaries on the *ahadith* or passages from the Qur'an, all liberally interspersed with discourses on aspects of Sufi teaching. While the *Mathnawi* was still being written, it came in for criticism from those who were looking for a more readily recognizable treatise on the Sufi Path or a scholarly exposition of profound esoteric truths. Rumi's response to his critic offers helpful guidance to the modern reader who may be taking up the *Mathnawi* for the first time, for in it Rumi reminds us that the outer form of a thing can veil its essential meaning. If, like Rumi's critic, we allow ourselves to become caught up in the form of the *Mathnawi*, the meaning will remain concealed behind its veil of words.

> Even before this story reaches its conclusion, the foul stench of envy wafts in my direction. I'm not bothered by this, though such a kick might make a simple-hearted mind falter. The sage of Ghazna [Sana'i] captured so well the spiritual likeness of those who are veiled and see the Qur'anic text as nothing but words (which is not surprising since they have gone astray). 'A blind person's eye perceives only the heat from the illuminating rays of the sun.'

All of a sudden, an ass sticks his head out of his stable and, braying like an old crone, says, 'This work' (he means the *Mathnawi*) 'is poor, the story of the Prophet retold, nothing more. It has no discussion of those profound mysteries towards which the saints gallop in haste, nor of the stations from asceticism to self-effacement which lead step by step to union with God. It lacks any explanation of the stages and stations, those wings by which the mystic soars on high.'

When the Book of God [the Qur'an] came down, the unbelievers dismissed it in the same way, saying, 'It is nothing but legends and paltry tales, lacking any profound inquiry or lofty speculation, so that even little children can understand – a list of dos and don'ts, tales of Joseph and his curly locks, of Jacob, and of Zulaykha and her love. It is plain, and easily understood by every one. Where is any exposition that would mystify the intellect?' [Through Muhammad] God said, 'If this seems easy to you, then write one surah that is equally easy. Let men and the jinn and those among you who are skilled in writing produce just one "easy" verse.'

Know that the words of the Qur'an are simple, but under the outward sense is an inner meaning, and under this inner meaning is a third wherein the intellect becomes mystified. The fourth meaning of the Qur'an has been seen by no one but God, the Incomparable, the Self-Sufficient. My son, don't read only the outward meaning of the Qur'an, like Iblis who saw Adam as only clay. The outward Qur'an is like the human body, for its form is visible while its spirit is hidden . . .

O critical dog! You are doing a lot of noisome barking . . . But I will follow the advice of the Sage of Ghazna: I will not allow myself to be affected by these taunts . . . Does a caravan ever turn back from a journey because of the barking of dogs?

(M III: 4227–48, 4282, 4291; M VI: 12)

In the opening verses of Book VI, Rumi describes the *Mathnawi* from his own point of view. In so doing, he offers us helpful guidance for our reading of it, encouraging us to engage with its deeper meaning.

> If your thirst is for the Ocean, dig a hole in the island of the *Mathnawi*. Dig such a deep hole in it that in every moment you see it only as spiritual. When the wind blows away the straw from the surface of the river, the water reveals itself to be of one colour. Look at the branches of coral, newly-formed! Look at the fruits growing in the waters of the spirit! When the words and sounds of the *Mathnawi* are swept away, it becomes the Ocean. Then speaker and hearer and the words themselves become one.
>
> (M VI: 67–72)

The man who swallowed a snake

In the following tale, the wise man can be equated with the Sufi shaykh, and the sleeping man with our unenlightened state. The beating the sleeping man receives is an allegory for the suffering that we experience as we awaken to reality.

> One day a wise man was riding along the road when he came across a man who was fast asleep. As he passed by, he saw a snake sliding into the sleeping man's mouth. The wise man dismounted quickly and tried to scare the snake away, but to no avail. Taking up his club, he struck the sleeping man with several powerful blows. Awakened abruptly from his sleep, the man fled for safety to a nearby tree. It was an apple tree, and the ground around it was covered with rotting fruit. 'Eat them!' ordered the wise man, stuffing the mouth of the terrified man with apples until no more would go in.
>
> 'Why are you doing this to me?' spluttered the man. 'What have I done to offend you? If you have a deep-seated quarrel with me, settle it with your sword! Oh, cursed was the hour that you first saw me, and blessed is

the man who never sets eyes on you! No guilt, no sin, not the slightest misdemeanour – even heretics wouldn't approve of punishment this severe. Look! My mouth is pouring with blood and words! O God, I beg Thee, repay him in like manner!' Yet however much the man cursed, the wise man continued to shower him with blows.

'Keep running!' shouted the wise man, and the man kept running from his pursuer, picking himself up off the ground whenever he fell flat on his face. Stuffed with apples, his body covered in cuts and bruises, he was chased backwards and forwards by the wise man until nightfall when he was seized by a violent bout of vomiting. Everything came up, including the snake.

When the man saw the ugly black reptile, he forgot all about the beating he had received and fell on his knees at the feet of the man who had saved him. 'Truly,' he said, 'You are either Gabriel or God, for you are the lord of beneficence! Oh, blessed is the hour that you first saw me, for I was dead and you have given me new life . . . Had I known, how could I have said such foolish things? I would have praised you, had you given me the slightest hint as to what you were really doing. Instead, you kept quiet, and carried on beating me in silence.'

'Had I told you about the snake,' replied the wise man, 'you might have died of fright . . . You would have been so terrified that you would not have been able to eat, nor to vomit. I heard your abuse but carried on with what I had to do, repeating to myself, "O Lord, make it easy!"'

(M II: 1878–96, 1904–6, 1910, 1922–3)

To explain the reason for the wise man's seemingly strange behaviour, Rumi quotes the Prophet Muhammad, 'If I were to describe the true nature of the enemy within the human soul, even the bravest of men would lose hope. No one would do anything any more. They would not even have the strength of will to pray or fast. I therefore attend to your needs without speaking, so that the bird that has lost its feathers may regain its wings' (M II: 1911–12, 1917). 'This is the nature of the enmity of the wise,' says Rumi. Unlike the snake that poisons us from within, 'the venom of the wise brings joy to the soul' (M II: 1930).

The man who was befriended by a bear

Here Rumi offers us an alternative ending to the tale of the man who swallowed a snake, for the principal character ignores the advice of a concerned friend (the Sufi shaykh, or the man's higher self) and chooses to befriend a bear (his lower or animal self). Rumi leaves us in little doubt as to the outcome that awaits us if we make a similar choice.

> A brave man once rescued a bear from the jaws of a dragon. The bear was so grateful that it became the man's devoted companion, so much so that whenever he lay down to rest the bear would stand guard.
>
> One day a friend asked the man, 'Brother, what are you doing with this bear?'
>
> The man told him the story about the dragon, and how he had rescued the bear. 'Never trust a bear,' said the friend. 'For the friendship of a fool is worse than his enmity. You should drive it away and have nothing more to do with it.'
>
> 'I do believe he's jealous,' said the man to himself. Then, speaking aloud, he said to his friend, 'Ignore the fact he's a bear. Just look at his affection for me.'
>
> 'The affection of fools is seductive,' replied the friend. 'I'll help you to drive him off. Don't give up your real friends to become friends with a bear!'
>
> 'Go away,' said the man, 'It's none of your business what I do.'
>
> 'It is my business,' replied the friend. Taking the other man's hand, he continued, 'My concern for you is genuine. Don't go into the forest with such an animal. Beware of the bear!' But the man with the bear withdrew his hand. 'I'm leaving,' said the friend, 'since it's clear you intend going your own way.'

'Then leave!' shouted the man. 'Don't worry yourself on my account. And you can stop peddling all this advice, you interfering busybody!'

'Believe me,' answered the friend, 'I have no wish to antagonise you. It's just that it would be better for you if you came with me.'

'All this is making me tired,' responded the man. 'Now go, and leave me alone.'

'I beg you, follow the advice of your friend. That way you'll be able to sleep safely, for you'll be watched over by one who is wise in the ways of God.'

The earnestness of his friend's pleas set the man thinking, and he began to imagine all sorts of reasons for his friend's concern. 'Perhaps he's a murderer and he's going to attack me. Or perhaps he's a beggar hoping to sell me something. Or maybe he's made a bet with some friends that he can come between me and my bear.'

So the two men parted and went their separate ways: one to his house; the other with his bear to the forest, where he fell asleep. The bear watched over the sleeping man, and while he slept he drove away the flies from the man's face. But the flies returned. The bear drove them away several times, but the flies persisted in coming back. This so enraged the bear that he picked up a large rock, waited till the flies had settled on the man's face, and then hurled the rock at the flies. The rock smashed the man's face to pulp, which just goes to show, 'The love of a fool is like the love of a bear. For him, friendship is enmity, and enmity is friendship.'

(M II: 1970, 2010–31, 2124–30)

Dalqak comes to town

The King of Tirmid needed a courier to complete some urgent business in Samarkand. He sent out a proclamation offering a rich reward – a large sum of gold, robes of honour, slave-boys and slave-girls – to anyone who would go to Samarkand and back in five days.

Dalqak, the court jester, was out in the country when he heard the proclamation, and he immediately mounted his horse and set off for Tirmid at a furious gallop. He rode so hard and fast that two horses dropped dead from exhaustion along the way. Still covered with dust from his journey, he burst into the council chamber at an ungodly hour and demanded an immediate audience with the king, thus provoking rumours among the council members and giving the king cause for concern. The panic-stricken inhabitants of the city wondered what catastrophe could be imminent, saying, 'Why would Dalqak ride so hard that several horses died under him?' Such was the commotion caused by Dalqak's urgent arrival that the people's imaginations ran wild. Some said they were about to be attacked by a conquering army; others that some kind of Divine retribution was on its way. Fear drove them to gather at the king's palace.

Meanwhile, at the palace, Dalqak had been granted an immediate audience with the king. As the jester prostrated himself at the king's feet, the king asked, 'What on earth is the matter?' But Dalqak put his finger to his lips, as if to say, 'Hush!' When others echoed the king's question, he repeated the gesture. The tension mounted in his audience, who had never before seen the jester like this. The grave expression on his face increased their sense of apprehension and foreboding. Then Dalqak made another gesture, implying that he needed more time to get his breath back.

The suspense was such that a fearful dread struck the king, and his mouth went dry. It was the first time he had ever seen his jester in this state. Usually he was the best of company, telling stories and jokes until the king felt as though his sides were about to split from laughing. Sometimes he would make the king laugh so much that he fell off his throne, but the Dalqak who stood before him now was grim-faced and serious, and he kept putting his finger to his lips as though to say, 'Hush, Oh King!' The king's anxiety was heightened because he knew that the rulers of many kingdoms in the region had already been killed by the scheming governor of Khwarizmshah, and he was afraid of suffering the same fate. Dalqak's behaviour only served to increase his apprehension. 'Hurry up, Dalqak!' exclaimed the king. 'Why are you so flustered? Tell us what's the matter.'

'I was far out in the country,' began Dalqak, 'when I heard that the king needed someone to go to Samarkand and back in three days, and that whoever went would receive a rich reward. Well, I hurried back to tell you that I can't do it. I'm not fit enough, so please don't expect me to go.'

'Damn you and your hurry!' shouted the king. 'You've thrown the entire city into a state of total chaos just to tell me this? You crazy fool!'

(M VI: 2510–6)

Rumi then explains the allegorical meaning of this tale, in which Dalqak's behaviour typifies those spiritually immature people who make a great deal of noise about being on the Sufi Path.

[They say] 'We are travellers on the path to poverty and non-existence,' and boast of being a Sufi shaykh, and pretend to have attained a similar spiritual station to that of Bayazid Bistami! Claiming that they have abandoned their ego and achieved union with God, they set up a school for disciples under false pretences.

This state of affairs is comparable to a house in which the family of a bridegroom is in a state of turmoil over a forthcoming marriage about which neither the girl nor her family know anything. The bridegroom's family says, 'We've done everything on our side to make ready for the bride.' Has any message come from the girl's house? 'No.' Not even a little bird? 'No.' After all those letters you've sent out, one after the other, have you received no response from the neighbour's house? 'No, but the Friend knows of the matter because He can read what is in our hearts.' Why, then, have you received no answer from the Friend, the object of your hope? He has given you a hundred signs, both outwardly and inwardly. But let's say no more on the subject. We have exposed their hypocrisy enough.

(M VI: 2510–57)

The Pear Tree

In Book IV of the *Mathnawi*, Rumi tells the following bawdy story about a woman who exploits the hallucinatory properties attributed to the pear tree in order to cuckold her husband:

A certain woman was overcome with a desire to make love with her lover in the presence of her half-witted husband. So she said to her spouse, 'I'm going to climb the tree and gather some fruit.' But when she had climbed to the top of the tree she looked down in her husband's direction, burst into tears, and railed at him, 'You sordid creature! Who is that fellow lying on top of you? You're letting him hump you like a woman. Oh, husband. You're little better than a eunuch.'

'Are you out of your mind?' replied the husband. 'There's no one down here but me.' But the wife repeated her accusation, 'Do you think from up here I can't see what you're up to with that man lying on top of you?'

'Listen, wife,' said the husband. 'Come down from the tree. You're clearly losing your mind.'

The woman came down from the tree, and when her husband had climbed up she took her lover in her arms. Her husband called out in protest, 'You whore! Who is that you're riding?'

'What!' cried out the wife. 'Don't talk such rubbish. There's nobody here but me.'

The husband repeated his accusation. 'Well, you cuckold,' said the wife. 'It must be to do with the pear-tree. When I was up there I saw things just as falsely as you. Now, come on down so that you can see nothing is going on. The pear-tree is the cause of the illusion. From the top of the pear-tree I saw things just as falsely as you.'

(M IV: 3544–57)

Similar bawdy stories involving the alleged hallucinatory properties of pear trees appeared in the collections of tales of low life that circulated orally throughout medieval Europe – a literary genre known by the French name of *fabliaux*. The inclusion of the pear tree story in European works illustrates the cultural cross-pollination that took place between the Islamic and European worlds in the Middle Ages. A version of the story appears in the *Decameron*, by Giovanni Boccaccio (1313–75), a work that was probably begun in about 1350, some eighty or so years after the death of Rumi. It appears again in the Merchant's Tale in Chaucer's *Canterbury Tales*, written sometime after 1370. Chaucer's *Parliament of the Fowls* also bears a strong resemblance to *The Conference of the Birds*, written by the Persian Sufi poet and mystic Fariduddin Attar (d.1220/9). Whereas both Boccaccio's and Chaucer's versions of the pear tree tale end with the duping of the cuckolded husband, Rumi concludes his rendering of the story by informing us that even amusing stories such as this are a means of instruction. Outlining a principle that still holds good with modern 'Sufi jokes', such as those featuring the character known as Hodja or Mulla Nasruddin, Rumi advises us to listen to them 'in earnest'. As he points out, 'to jesters every earnest matter is a jest; to the wise all jests are earnest' (M IV: 3559).

Lazy people look for the pear-tree, but they have far to go before they reach the other pear-tree. Come down from your present pear-tree, for it has made you incapable of seeing straight. Your pear-tree is that base egoism which causes you to believe in your own self-existence and to see everything awry and topsy-turvy. When you have the humility to come down from this particular pear-tree, your thoughts, vision and words will no longer be distorted, for God will grant you clear-sightedness. You will see that God, in His mercy, has transformed it into a tree of abundance whose branches reach up to the heavens . . . In the shade of this tree, all your needs will be fulfilled. Such is the Divine alchemy.

(M IV: 3560–72)

When the wife is up in the pear tree in Rumi's version of the story, she accuses her husband of pederasty, of letting himself be 'humped like a woman' by the man on top of him. A verse from the *Divan* sheds some possible light on her accusation, which has nothing to do with the man's sexuality. Rumi writes, 'Oh, you who call yourself a man! What kind of manliness is this, letting Iblis [the devil] hump you like a pederast?' (D 717: Chittick, *The Sufi Path of Love*, p. 168). In this context, 'manliness' can be applied equally to a man or woman and is used metaphorically to describe a person who, having mastered his lower self, has attained a state of spiritual maturity. Conversely, 'woman' or 'pederast' are employed to denote those who are governed by the whims and desires of their lower or carnal self.

The Three Fish

One of the sources of Rumi's stories is the ancient collection of tales known as the *Fables of Bidpai*, or *Kalila and Dimna*, from which comes the story of the three fish. But, as Rumi says, the original story is just the husk: his own telling provides the 'spiritual kernel'.

There were once three large fish who lived in a lake: one wise, one clever, and one stupid. One day some fishermen passed the lake, and seeing the three big fish they hurried off to fetch their nets. But the fish saw them, and their sixth sense told them of the men's intention. Wise fish decided that it was time to leave the lake and head for the ocean, even though the journey would be difficult. Having made up his mind to leave the lake, he said to himself, 'I won't discuss this with the others in case they try to dissuade me and thus weaken my resolve. They love their home too much to want to leave it, and some of their reluctance might rub off on me.' . . .

So, without consulting the others, he left the lake and swam resolutely on until he reached the safe haven of the boundless ocean. He suffered much along the way, but his determination to keep going until he reached his goal was similar to that of a deer pursued by hounds: to save itself from being caught it will run and run until it can run no more.

In the meantime, the fishermen returned to the lake with their nets. When clever fish saw the men come back, he began to scold himself. 'I've lost a good friend, who has escaped disaster by heading for the ocean,' he said to himself as he swam around in the depths of the lake. 'I should have followed his example. Still, there's no point in regretting what has happened. I can't undo the past . . . I'll have to look after myself from hereon, and I'll begin by pretending to be dead. I'll turn over and float belly-up on the water. I'll allow myself to drift, the way water weeds do, rather than swim. I will die, for to die before dying is to be relieved of suffering.' So saying, he rolled over and allowed the water to carry him up to the surface of the lake.

The fishermen voiced their annoyance when they saw clever fish floating on the surface, saying, 'Alas, the best fish is dead.'

When he heard the men say 'Alas', clever fish said to himself, 'My plan has worked, and I have been spared.'

One of the fishermen grabbed hold of clever fish, spat on him, and threw him onto the ground. Without waiting any longer, clever fish rolled over and over until he reached the stream that led to the ocean.

Meanwhile stupid fish swam frantically up and down the lake in an effort to save himself. When the fishermen cast their net, he swam straight into it. He realized the

extent of his folly as he lay sizzling in the frying pan over a
hot fire, and said to himself, 'If I ever get out of this, I will
never again live in a lake. Instead, I'll make my home in the
ocean, where I can live in safety for ever more.'

(M IV: 2204–8, 2235–44, 2268–85)

Rumi prepares the ground for our understanding of the story of the
three fish with an explanation of the three types of people represented
in the tale: the intelligent, the half-intelligent and those totally lacking
in intelligence (*see* 'Two kinds of intelligence', page 167). The
intelligent person can be equated with the Sufi shaykh, whose
enlightened state serves as a lamp to light the way for his followers.
Rumi advises us to entrust ourselves to his guidance, like the half-
intelligent person, who regards the intelligent person as the eye by
which he sees. By clinging to him in the way that a blind person clings
to a guide, he too develops the capacity to see. The third type is the
ass who has not one gram of intelligence. Possessing no intelligence of
his own, he rejects the guidance offered by those who are more
enlightened than himself. Whereas the half-intelligent person 'dies' to
the self (achieves self-annihilation or *fana*'), the ass is considered to be
dead spiritually. Lacking guidance from both within and without, he
wanders first in one direction, then in another, wherever his lower self
leads him.

When the intelligent fish resolves to undertake the long journey
to the ocean, he decides not to consult the other two fish lest their
unwillingness to leave the home they love weakens his resolve. Rumi
explains his decision thus, 'If you are a traveller [on the Path], take
counsel from fellow travellers rather than stay-at-homes. True, the
hadith says, "Love of one's country is part of the Faith", but beyond the
literal interpretation there is an inner meaning to the expression
"loving one's country"' (M IV: 2208–10). As the action of the intelligent
fish demonstrates, our true country is the Ocean of Being.

The symbolic imagery of the story of the three fish is found in a
number of Rumi's odes from the *Divan*. The different form of

expression leads the poet to make his point more succinctly, as evidenced in the following examples, the first of which expands on the water imagery while explaining the real reason for the hasty departure of the intelligent fish. The references to 'heaven and earth' in the opening lines point to the duality of the formal or phenomenal world. The second example explains the course of action taken by the half-intelligent fish, while the third is relevant to the predicament in which the stupid fish finds himself at the end of the story.

> Heaven and earth are like a jug and bucket; water is
>   outside heaven and earth.
> Make haste to depart from heaven and earth, and see
>   water flowing from placelessness,
> Let the fish of your soul escape this pool and drink the
>   water of the boundless ocean.
> In that ocean the fish are all like Khidr: immortal fish,
>   immortal water.

> (D 294: A1:33)

> Why shouldn't a fish leap easily from dry land into the
>   water,
> when it hears the call of the waves from the limpid ocean?

> (D 1353: A:167)

> At once sinful and penitent,
> I'm like a fish in the pan –
> burning first on one side,
> then on the other.

> (D 1463: A:179)

The maidservant, the ass, and the gourd

Several passages in the tales told in the *Mathnawi* contain sexually explicit language, and when Professor Nicholson translated Rumi's book into English he saw fit to translate these passages into Latin. In the following version of the tale of the maidservant, the ass, and the gourd, these passages have been rendered into English.

A lady's maid had trained an ass to perform the sexual functions of a man. Using a gourd, she had made a device to prevent the ass's penis from penetrating too far during intercourse: had the whole of the ass's member gone into her, it would have wreaked havoc in her womb and intestines. The maid, who had fashioned the gourd to perfection, gained much satisfaction from the arrangement and enjoyed herself so often that the ass began to lose weight. The mistress of the house was puzzled as to why the ass was looking thin, so she took him to the blacksmith and asked, 'What sickness has caused this ass to become so thin?' As the blacksmith was unable to help, she decided to investigate the matter for herself. Then one day, through a crack in the door, she saw the little narcissus lying under the ass. It was mounting her in exactly the same way as a man takes a woman. Marvelling at the size of the ass's member, she said to herself, 'Since this is possible, I have the greater right since it is my ass. It has been perfectly trained: the table has been laid and the lamp is lit.' Pretending to have seen nothing, she knocked on the door, calling to the maid to open. The maid hid the gourd and, taking up a broom in her hand, opened the door, pretending she had been cleaning the room.

'You cunning vixen,' said the mistress under her breath. 'You've put on a prim face and picked up a broom, depriving the ass of his food.' Concealing her lust, the mistress acted the innocent, sent the maid on an errand, closed the door behind her, and said, 'Now I can enjoy myself in private.' . . .

The maid went on her errand, thinking to herself, 'O mistress, you've sent the expert away. You were too embarrassed to ask me about the device of the gourd, and without my expert knowledge you will foolishly put your life at risk.' . . .

But the fire of passion was lit in her mistress, whose vagina was now singing like a nightingale. Dizzy with excitement, she set a chair as she had seen the maid do, and lay down under the ass. She raised her legs and drew him into her. The ass's member fanned the flames of her desire, and as she urged him on the ass obligingly pushed himself further into her, right up to his testicles. He tore into her intestines, and without uttering a word she died. The chair fell in one direction, she in the other. The room was smeared with blood, and the woman lay prostrate on the floor. O reader, have you ever seen anyone make a martyr of themselves for an ass? . . .

When the maid returned, she saw her dead mistress lying under the ass. 'O stupid woman!' she said. 'Look what has happened to you. You saw only the outward appearance of what I did and my secret remained hidden from you. You went into business without mastering the tricks of the trade! Either you only saw the ass's member which appeared so sweet and tempting that you didn't see the gourd, or you were so enamoured of the ass that the gourd remained hidden from your sight.'

(M V: 1333–62, 1403–4, 1382–90, 1417–22)

To ensure that we are left in no doubt as to his purpose in telling this tale, Rumi explains that 'the male ass is the animal or carnal self: to be under it is more shameful than the behaviour of that woman. If you are a martyr to your carnal self, you are acting just like her' (M V 1392–3). The woman's greed for the ass was her undoing, whereas the maid had mastered the art of intercourse with the carnal self, using it to her own ends rather than becoming a martyr to it. Moreover, having mastered it, her ass grew thin and was becoming like the lean ass of Jesus (*see* page 122).

Chapter Ten

Odes from the *Divan-i Shams-i Tabrizi*

My poetry is like Egyptian bread: night passes, and you
can no longer eat it.
Eat it while it is still fresh, before the dust settles on it.

(D 981: A1/125)

IF THERE IS NO TURNING . . .

According to Aflaki, Rumi composed this poem after attending prayers
with a group of followers at the congregational mosque at Meram, on
the outskirts of Konya. When prayers were over, Rumi made his way to
a nearby mill. His followers found him whirling around in an ecstatic
dance. Rumi exclaimed, 'This mill-stone is saying, "Glorious and Holy
is He!"', and then proceeded to recite the poem.

The heart is like grain, we are like the mill.
How does the mill know why it turns?
The body's the mill-stone, the water its thoughts;
The stone says, 'The water knows its course!'
The water says, 'Ask the miller, he's the one
    who sends this water cascading down.'
The miller says, 'If there is no turning,
    O bread-eater, there will be no dough.'
Turn, and turn again. Silence!
Ask God, He will tell you.

(D 181: A1:21)

'WHO IS AT THE DOOR?'

He asked, 'Who is at the door?'
    I said, 'Your humble slave.'
He said, 'What is your business?'
    I said, 'My Lord, to greet you.'
He said, 'How long will you knock?'
    I said, 'Until you answer.'
He said, 'How long will you cook?'
    I said, 'Until I am resurrected.'
Laying claim to love, I swore many oaths
    renouncing position and power.
He warned, 'The judge will require proof of your claim.'
    I said, 'My tears are proof, so is my pallid face.'
He said, 'Your evidence is unacceptable.
    Your proof is both vague and corrupted.'
I said, 'By your supreme justice,
    their witness is both just and true.'
He said, 'Who accompanied you here?'
    I said, 'O Lord, the image I have of you.'
He said, 'Who summoned you here?'
    I said, 'The fragrance of your cup.'
He said, 'What are you seeking?'
    I said, 'Fidelity and friendship.'
He said, 'What do you want from me?'
    I said, 'Your universal grace.'
He said, 'Where is the most agreeable place?'
    I said, 'In the palace of the Emperor.'
He said, 'What did you see there?'
    I said, 'A hundred marvels.'
He said, 'Then why is it so wretched?'
    I said, 'For fear of thieves and robbers.'
He said, 'Who are the thieves?'
    I said, 'Recrimination and blame.'
He said, 'And where can one find safety?'
    I said, 'In abstinence and piety.'
He said, 'What is abstinence?'
    I said, 'The way to salvation.'

He said, 'Where is tribulation?'
    I said, 'On the path of Your love.'
He said, 'How do you travel?'
    I said, 'With perseverance.'
Silence! If I say any more
    you will be completely lost,
    with no home to call your own.

(D 436: A1:50)

THOU AND I

Blessed is the moment when we sit side by side, thou and I.
    Two forms and two faces, but just one soul, thou and I.
The scent of flowers and the birdsong will be a fountain
    of life for us, as we stroll in the garden, thou and I.
The stars up above will gaze down on us,
    and we'll show them the crescent moon, thou and I.
Thou and I, devoid of self, shall be mingled in ecstasy,
    full of joy and free from idle chatter, thou and I.
Sugar-chewing birds of paradise will eat their hearts out
    in the place we fill with laughter, thou and I.
The miracle is this: thou and I, seated in the same spot,
    are at this moment in Iraq and Khorasan, thou and I.
We, who are in one form in this world,
    are in another form in sweet eternity, thou and I.

(D 2214: A2:280)

THE INTELLECTUAL AND THE LOVER

The intellectual is always showing off;
    The lover is always losing his self.
The intellectual runs away, afraid of the water;
    Love is all about drowning in the ocean.
Intellectuals devise ways to repose;
    Lovers find no comfort in rest.
The lover is always alone, even when with others:

like oil floating on water, the two do not mix.
The one who seeks to advise a lover
    gains nothing. He is passion's fool.
Love, like musk, is reputed for its scent.
    Can musk escape its reputation?
Love is like a tree, and lovers are its shade;
    the shade spreads far, but can never quit the tree.
To be an intellectual, a child must grow old,
    whereas love gives old men back their youth.

(D 1957: A2:241)

THIS IS LOVE . . .

This is love: to soar towards the heavens,
    every moment, to tear aside a hundred veils.
The first move, to let go of life.
    The last step, to walk without feet.
To regard this world as invisible,
    and to disregard the eye of the self.

'O heart,' I said, 'you are blessed
    to enter this circle of lovers,
    to see beyond what eye can see,
    to enter the windings of the breast.
O soul, how did you begin to breathe?
O heart, how did you begin to beat?
O soul-bird, speak the language of birds,
    for I understand your hidden meaning.'

My soul replied, 'I was in the Workshop
    the day this house of water and clay was fired.
I was fleeing from the phenomenal world,
    even while it was being created.
When I could resist no more, I was dragged down,
    and, like a ball of clay, I was moulded into form.

(D 1919: A2:237)

LOVERS, IT IS TIME TO FORSAKE THE WORLD

O lovers, lovers, it is time to forsake the world:
heaven's departure drum is sounding in my soul's ear.

The camel driver has risen, made ready the caravan,
and asks us to forgive him: 'O travellers, why are you
asleep?'

All around us are the sounds of departure and camel
bells; at every moment a soul and a spirit leaves for the
Placeless.

The stars shine like candles behind a deep-blue veil,
and a wondrous people issues forth to make the invisible
visible.

You have been in a deep sleep beneath the turning
spheres; Be warned! Sleep is heavy but life is light and
brief.

O heart, go seek the Beloved! O friend, seek the
Friend! O watchman, wake up! A watchman is not here
to sleep.

Everywhere there is noise and movement, candles and
torches; for tonight this pregnant world gives birth to the
Eternal.

You were clay, now you are spirit; ignorant, now
wise. That which has drawn you this far will draw you
yet further.

As He draws you to Himself, how sweet your
suffering becomes; His fires are like water; do not be
troubled by them.

His mission is to dwell in the heart and break your
vows of contrition. Through His diverse designs, these
atoms tremble to the core.

O arrogant fool, jumping up from your hole to cry 'I
am lord of all'. How long will you remain jumped-up?
Bow down, or else be bowed.

You have nurtured the seeds of hypocrisy and
indulged in derision. You denied the existence of Truth,
you whoremonger!

Like an ass, you crave for straw; like a cauldron, you are black; you are better off at the bottom of a well, you disgusting creature.

Within me there is Another who makes my eyes spark; If water scalds, it is because of the fire. Let this be known!

I have no stone in my hand; I have no quarrel with anyone; I rebuke no one, for I possess the sweetness of the rose garden.

My eye is from that Source, from another world. One world here, another there – I am sitting on the threshold.

Only those on the threshold know the eloquence of silence. Enough has been said. Say no more. Hold the tongue.

(D 1789: A2:222)

I AM A PAINTER, A PICTURE-MAKER . . .

I am a painter, a picture-maker.
Every moment I create beautiful idols,
but in your presence I erase them all.

I conjure up a hundred images and fill them with spirit,
but when I behold your image
I throw them in the fire.

Are you the winemaker's cup-bearer,
or the enemy of every sober man?
or is it you who lays to ruin every house I build?

My soul pours forth and mingles with yours.
Because my soul bears your fragrance,
I will cherish my soul.

Every drop of blood I spill tells the earth,
'The Beloved and I are of one colour,
we are conjoined in love.'

In this house of clay and water,
my heart lies waste without you;
Enter this house, my Beloved, or I will leave it.

(D 1462: A1:178))

IF MY WORDS ARE NOT WORTHY OF YOUR LIPS . . .
Rumi was aware of the inadequacy of words as an expression of
Divine Truth. In spite of this, the state of ecstatic union in which he
found himself was frequently so overwhelming that, like Hallaj and
Bayazid before him, he was unable to restrain himself from verbal
expression. The following poem, which opens with Rumi questioning
the Friend as to whether his words are a true expression of the
Divine, spells out the poet's dilemma. (The 'bolbol' referred to in
line 16 is the nightingale.)

If my words are not worthy of Your lips,
    take up a rock and crush my mouth.
When a child spouts nonsense, doesn't a loving mother
    prick his lips to make him speak sense?
To preserve the Majesty of Your lips, burn and tear
    to pieces two hundred mouths and worlds.
When a thirsty man runs to the shore,
    the waves hold a sword to his throat.
I'm like the lily which, having seen Your garden,
    is put to shame: it wilts and its tongue is stilled.
But I'm also like a tambourine: when Your hand
    strikes me, I open my mouth and call out.
Don't put me down before the crescendo;
    lift up Your hem from the dust of this world.
We may be drunk from beholding the rose, but the sweet
    song of the bolbol fills Your rose garden.
Joseph's beauty may be greatest when he is naked,
    yet it's the sight of his shirt that opens our eyes.
Though our origin is the glittering sun of the soul,
    no one ever reached that heaven without a body.

Silence! Even if the corpse-washer binds my jaw shut,
   you'll still hear this refrain after I'm gone.

                                        (D 2083: A2:260)

I HAVE RELINQUISHED DUALITY . . .

What am I to do, O Muslims? for I no longer recognize
   myself.
I am neither Christian, nor Jew, nor Magian, nor Muslim.
I am not of the East nor of the West, not of the land nor
   the sea;
I am not from nature's mine, nor from the circling
   spheres.
I am not of earth, nor water, nor wind nor fire.
I am not of the heavens, nor dust, nor existence, nor
   entity.
I am not of India nor China, not of Bulghar, nor Saqsin;
I am not of the kingdom of Iraquain, nor the land of
   Khorasan.
I am not of this world, nor the next, not of Paradise nor
   Hell;
I am not of Adam, nor Eve, not of Eden nor Rizwan.
My place is the Placeless, my trace is the Traceless;
I am neither body nor soul, for I belong to the soul of the
   Beloved.
I have relinquished duality and seen the two worlds as one;
One I seek, One I know, One I see, One I call.
He is the First, He is the Last, He is the Outward, He is
   the Inward;
I know of nothing but *Hu* [He], and none besides He
   Who Is.
Intoxicated with the cup of Love, the two worlds slip
   from my hands.
Now I have nothing to do but carousing and celebration.
If I so much as pass one moment of my life without You,
I will repent my whole life from that moment on.
If I so much as win one moment in this world with You,

I will trample the two worlds underfoot in a never-ending
    dance of joy.
O Shams of Tabriz, in this world I am so intoxicated
that apart from drunkenness and celebration I have no
    tale to tell.

(after Nicholson, *Selected Poems
from the Divan-i Shams-i Tabrizi*, p. 31)

GO LAY YOUR HEAD ON A PILLOW . . .

Aflaki recounts that, as Rumi lay on his deathbed, Sultan Walad would
not leave his father's side. Rumi assured his distraught son that he was
feeling better, and sent him away to get some rest. When his son had
left, Rumi began to recite this poem.

Go lay your head on a pillow, son, let me be alone;
    leave me ruined, exhausted from this night journey,
    writhing in a wave of passion until the dawn.
If you will, stay and have mercy; if you will, leave and be
    cruel.
Take flight, lest you share in this affliction;
    choose the path of safety, not tribulation.
We have crept into this grieving corner,
    turning the mill-wheel with our flow of tears.

The tyrant with a heart of stone is killing me,
    yet no one says, 'Prepare to pay the blood-money.'
The lord of those with lovely faces is not duty-bound to
    be faithful, but be steadfast, pale lover, and endure.
The sole cure for this pain is dying,
    and so why would I say, 'Cure this pain'?

Last night I dreamt of an old man standing in the garden
    of love, he beckoned with his hand, and said, 'Come
    towards me.'
If a dragon blocks the path, Love works like an emerald –
    its radiance repels dragons.

But enough! I am losing my self.
 If you would be a man of superior learning,
 quote the history book of Bu 'Ali,
 and berate that so-and-so, Bu 'Ala.

(D 2039: A2:253)

In folklore, it was believed that the shimmering green of the emerald had the power to blind serpents and dragons. The closing lines of the poem have a touch of irony about them. Here the name Bu 'Ali is a reference to Abu 'Ali ibn Sina (d.1037), known in the West as the philosopher Avicenna, while Bu 'Ala is taken to be Abu 'Ala al-Ma'arri (d.1057), the Syrian philosopher and poet. For Rumi, philosophers represented the partial intellect which is inferior to the Universal Intellect. According to A.J. Arberry, Rumi transposes the two men, a point that heightens the irony of these closing lines. (Arberry, *Mystical Poems of Rumi 2*, pp. 156–7)

ON THE DAY I DIE . . .

On the day I die, as my casket is being carried away,
 don't think it pains me to leave this world.
Don't weep for me; don't wail, 'Alas!'
 Don't fall into the devil's snare, that would be sad
 indeed.
When you see my cortège, don't say, 'He's parting!'
 For me, it is the moment of meeting and reunion.
As you bury me in the earth, don't say, 'Good-bye!'
 For the grave is a veil over union in Paradise.
When you see the lowering down, think of the rising up.
 When did setting ever lessen the sun or the moon?
What seems a setting to you is but a rising.
 The tomb may seem a prison, but it is freedom for
 the soul.
What seed is buried in the ground and doesn't grow?
 Why therefore do you doubt this human seed?
What bucket is lowered and doesn't come up filled?
 Why would this Joseph-Spirit resent the well?

When you close your mouth on this side, open it on the
    other and let your song echo through the air of the
    void.

(D 911: A1:118)

HOW WONDERFUL THE WAY YOU LEFT THIS WORLD

At last you've departed and gone to the Unseen.
    How wonderful the way you left this world.
You opened your wings, broke out of your cage,
    and took off for the world of the soul.
A favoured falcon, caged up by old woman world,
    but when you heard the falcon drum, you escaped to
    the Placeless.
A love-sick nightingale among owls,
    when the scent of roses reached you, you flew to the
    rose garden.
This tainted wine gave you a hangover,
    but now you've gone to Eternity's tavern.
Like a well-aimed arrow, you sped from this bow
    and flew straight for the target of bliss.
This spirit-snatching world tried to lead you astray with
    false signs, but you ignored them; instead, you left for
    the Signless.
Now you are the sun, what use is a crown?
    Now you've gone from the middle, what need of a
    belt?
I hear tales of those who gaze on the soul with blind eyes.
    Why soul-gaze when you are from the Soul of souls?
O heart, what a rare bird you are! In your quest for the
    Divine, you took off and flew straight to the spear-
    point like a shield.
The rose flees when autumn comes, but you –
    O fearless rose – dallied in the autumn wind.
You fell like rain from heaven on this worldly roof,
    and ran in all directions until you escaped down the
    gutter.

Be silent, and thus free from the pain of speech.
Don't go to sleep, now that you're in the arms of the
    Friend.

(D 3051: A2:395)

Bibliography

Aflaki, Shamsuddin Ahmed, *Manâqib al-'ârifin* (for English translation, *see* Redhouse, *Legends of the Sufis*)

Baldock, John, *The Essence of Sufism*, Eagle Editions, Royston, 2004

Bayrak, Shaykh Tosun, *The Most Beautiful Names*, Threshold Books, Putney, VT, 1985

Chittick, William C., *The Sufi Path of Love: The Spiritual Teachings of Rumi*, State University of New York Press, Albany, 1983

Danner, Victor, *The Islamic Tradition*, Amity House, Warwick, NY, 1988

Helminski, Kabir, *The Knowing Heart: A Sufi Path of Transformation*, Shambhala, Boston, MA, 2000

Hujwiri, *Kashf al-Mahjub ('The Revelation of the Veiled', an early Persian Treatise on Sufism)*, (trans. R.A. Nicholson, 1911), Gibb Memorial Trust, Warminster, 2000

Iqbal, Afzal, *The Life and Work of Jalal-ud-din Rumi*, Octagon Press, London, 1983

Khosla, K., *The Sufism of Rumi*, Element Books, Shaftesbury, 1987

Lewis, Franklin D., *Rumi – Past and Present, East and West: The Life, Teaching and Poetry of Jalâl al-Din Rumi*, Oneworld, Oxford, 2003

Lings, Martin, *What is Sufism?*, The Islamic Texts Society, Cambridge, 1999

McEvedy, Colin, *The Penguin Atlas of Medieval History*, Penguin, London, 1961

Nicholson, R.A., *Rumi: Poet and Mystic*, George Allen & Unwin, London, 1950

Redhouse, James W., *Legends of the Sufis: Selected Anecdotes from the Work Entitled 'The Acts of the Adepts'*, Theosophical Publishing House, 1976

Rumi, Jalaluddin, *Dīvānī Shamsi Tabrīzī*, English translations:

— *Mystical Poems of Rumi 1: First Selection, Poems 1–200*, (trans. A.J. Arberry), Chicago University Press, 1991

— *Mystical Poems of Rumi 2: Second Selection, Poems 201–400*, (trans. A.J. Arberry), Chicago University Press, 1991

— *Selected Poems from the Dīvānī Shamsī Tabrīzī*, (trans. R.A. Nicholson), Cambridge University Press, 1952

— *Where Two Oceans Meet: A Selection of Odes from the Divan of Shems of Tabriz*, (trans. James G. Cowan), Element Books, Shaftesbury, 1992

Rumi, Jalaluddin. *Fīhi māfīhi*, English translations:

— *Discourses of Rumi*, (trans. A.J. Arberry), Samuel Weiser, New York, 1972

— *Signs of the Unseen: The Discourses of Jalaluddin Rumi*, (trans. W.M. Thackston, Jr.), Shambhala, Boston, MA, 1999

Rumi, Jalaluddin. *Mathnawi*, English translations:

— *Masnavi i Ma'navi – The Spiritual Couplets of Maulána Jalálu-'d-Dín Muhammad i Rúmí* (abridged, trans. E.H. Whinfield, 1887) – recent editions of Whinfield's translation have been published by Octagon Press (London, 1979) and Watkins Publishing (London, 2002)

— *The Mathnawī of Jalālu'ddin Rumi*, (trans. R.A. Nicholson), E.J. Gibb Memorial Trust, Cambridge, 1982

— *Tales of Mystic Meaning: Selections from the Mathnawī of Jalāl-ud-Dīn Rumī*, (trans. Reynold A. Nicholson), Oneworld, Oxford, 1995

— *Delicious Laughter: Rambunctious Teaching Stories from the*

Mathnawī, (versions by Coleman Barks), Maypop Books, Athens, GA, 1990

— *Rumi: One-Handed Basket Weaving – Poems on the Theme of Work*, (versions by Coleman Barks) Maypop Books, Athens, GA, 1991

— *This Longing: Poetry, Teaching Stories, and Letters of Rumi*, (trans. Coleman Barks and John Moyne), Threshold Books, Putney, VT, 1988 – in addition to passages from the *Mathnawī*, this book contains 17 letters from the *Maktubāt*, a collection of 147 of Rumi's letters

Rumi, Jalaluddin, Editions containing translations and/or versions from two or more of the above works:

— *Love is a Stranger: Selected Lyric Poetry of Jelauddin Rumi*, (trans. Kabir Helminski), Threshold Books, Putney, VT, 1993

— *Rumi: A Spiritual Treasury*, (compiled by Juliet Mabey), Oneworld, Oxford, 2000

— *The Rumi Collection: an anthology of translations of Mevlâna Jalâluddin Rumi*, (ed. Kabir Helminski), Shambhala, Boston, MA, 2000

Schimmel, Annemarie, *Rumi's World: The Life and Work of the Great Sufi Poet*, Shambhala, Boston, 2001 (first published as *I Am Wind, You Are Fire*, 1992)

Shah, Idries, '*The Sufis*, Anchor, New York, 1971

— *The Way of the Sufi*, Arkana, London, 1990

Index